D1644173

Marks and Spencer p.l.c.
PO Box 3339
Chester CH99 9QS

shop online
www.marksandspencer.com

ISBN: 978-1-84805-439-4

Printed in China

Designed by Pink Creative

The views expressed in this book are those of the author but they are general views only and readers are urged to consult a relevant and qualified specialist for individual advice in particular situations. Marks and Spencer p.l.c. and Exclusive Editions Limited hereby exclude all liability to the extent permitted by law for any errors or omissions in this book and for any loss, damage or expense (whether direct or indirect) suffered by a third party relying on any information contained in this book.

NOTES FOR THE READER
This book uses both metric and imperial measurements. Follow the same units of measurement throughout; do not mix metric and imperial. All spoon measurements are level: teaspoons are assumed to be 5 ml, and tablespoons are assumed to be 15 ml. Unless otherwise stated, milk is assumed to be full fat, eggs and individual vegetables are medium, and pepper is freshly ground black pepper. The times given are an approximate guide only. Preparation times differ according to the techniques used by different people and the cooking times may also vary from those given. Optional ingredients, variations or serving suggestions have not been included in the calculations.

Recipes using raw or very lightly cooked eggs should be avoided by infants, the elderly, pregnant women, convalescents and anyone suffering from an illness. Pregnant and breastfeeding women are advised to avoid eating peanuts and peanut products. Sufferers from nut allergies should be aware that some of the ready-made ingredients used in the recipes in this book may contain nuts. Always check the packaging before use.

CONTENTS

INTRODUCTION

If you're the kind of person who cannot bear to eat bland or boring food and is keen to experiment in the kitchen with exotic herbs and spices, this is the perfect cookbook for you!

This fantastic collection contains over 100 recipes for all manner of spice sensations. Flick through the pages to find irresistible recipes for every taste and occasion – whether you fancy a dish that is delicately spiced or one with more of a flavour punch. From fiery Mexican-style dishes to bite-sized Spanish tapas, and from colourful Asian stir-fries to aromatic Moroccan tagines, there are meals inspired by cuisines across the globe. In fact, there is so much variety that you are guaranteed to find a recipe to satisfy your cravings for something spicy, whenever they strike!

SIZZLING

Snacks & light meals

NACHOS

Preheat the oven to 200°C/400°F/Gas Mark 6.

Spread the tortilla chips out over the base of a large, shallow ovenproof dish or roasting tin. Cover with the warmed refried beans. Scatter over the chillies and pimentos and season to taste with salt and pepper.

Mix the cheeses together in a bowl and sprinkle on top. Bake in the preheated oven for 5–8 minutes, or until the cheese is bubbling and melted. Serve immediately.

Serves 6

175 g/6 oz tortilla chips

400 g/14 oz canned refried beans, warmed

2 tbsp finely chopped bottled jalapeño chillies

200 g/7 oz canned or bottled pimentos or roasted peppers, drained and finely sliced

115 g/4 oz Gruyère cheese, grated

115 g/4 oz Cheddar cheese, grated

salt and pepper

FALAFEL

Soak the chickpeas overnight in enough cold water to cover them and allow room for expansion. Drain, then place in a saucepan, cover with fresh water and bring to the boil. Reduce the heat and simmer for 1 hour, or until tender. Drain.

Place the chickpeas in a food processor and blend to make a coarse paste. Add the onion, garlic, parsley, cumin, coriander, baking powder and cayenne pepper and salt to taste. Blend again to mix thoroughly.

Cover and leave to rest for 30 minutes, then shape into 8 balls. Leave to rest for a further 30 minutes. Heat the oil in a wok or large saucepan to 180–190°C/350–375°F, or until a cube of bread browns in 30 seconds. Gently drop in the balls and cook until golden brown. Remove from the oil and drain on a plate lined with kitchen paper.

Serve hot or at room temperature with hummus, tomato wedges and pitta bread. Garnish with parsley sprigs.

CHEESE & BEAN QUESADILLAS

To make the tomato salsa, stir all the ingredients together in a bowl and season to taste with salt. Cover with clingfilm and chill in the refrigerator until required.

Place the refried beans in a small pan and set over a low heat to warm through.

Meanwhile, make the tortillas pliable by warming each one gently in a lightly greased non-stick frying pan.

Remove the tortillas from the pan and quickly spread with a layer of warm beans. Sprinkle each tortilla with a little grated cheese, onion and coriander and top with a spoonful of the salsa. Roll up tightly.

Just before serving, heat the non-stick frying pan over a medium heat, sprinkling lightly with a couple of drops of water. Add the tortilla rolls, cover the pan and heat through until the cheese melts. Allow to brown lightly, if wished.

Remove the tortilla rolls from the pan and slice each roll, on the diagonal, into about 4 bite-sized pieces. Serve the quesadillas hot or cold, garnished with coriander leaves.

Serves 4–6

400 g/14 oz canned refried beans

8 flour tortillas

oil, for greasing

200 g/7 oz Cheddar cheese, grated

1 onion, chopped

½ bunch fresh coriander leaves, chopped, plus extra leaves to garnish

Tomato salsa

6–8 ripe tomatoes, finely chopped

about 100 ml/3½ fl oz tomato juice

3–4 garlic cloves, finely chopped

½ bunch fresh coriander leaves, roughly chopped

pinch of sugar

3–4 fresh green chillies, deseeded and finely chopped

½–1 tsp ground cumin

3–4 spring onions, finely chopped

salt

GUACAMOLE

Serves 4

2 large, ripe avocados

juice of 1 lime, or to taste

2 tsp olive oil

½ onion, finely chopped

1 fresh green chilli, such as poblano, deseeded and finely chopped

1 garlic clove, crushed

¼ tsp ground cumin

1 tbsp chopped fresh coriander, plus extra sprigs to garnish

salt and pepper

Cut the avocados in half lengthways and twist the halves in opposite directions to separate. Stab the stone with the point of a sharp knife and lift out.

Peel, then roughly chop the avocado halves and place in a non-metallic bowl. Squeeze over the lime juice and add the oil.

Mash the avocados with a fork to the desired consistency – either chunky or smooth. Mix in the onion, chilli, garlic, cumin and chopped coriander, then season to taste with salt and pepper.

Transfer to a serving dish and serve at once, to avoid discoloration, garnished with coriander sprigs.

ONION BHAJIS

Sift the besan flour, salt, cumin, turmeric, bicarbonate of soda and chilli powder into a large bowl. Add the lemon juice and the oil, then very gradually stir in just enough water until a batter similar in consistency to single cream forms. Mix in the onions and coriander seeds.

Heat enough oil for deep-frying in a wok, deep-fat fryer or large heavy-based saucepan to 180–190°C/350–375°F, or until a cube of bread browns in 30 seconds. Without overcrowding the pan, drop in spoonfuls of the onion mixture and fry for 2 minutes, then use tongs to flip the bhajis over and continue frying for a further 2 minutes, or until golden brown.

Immediately remove the bhajis from the oil and drain well on crumpled kitchen paper. Keep the bhajis warm while you continue frying the remaining batter. Serve hot.

Makes 12

140 g/5 oz besan or gram flour

1 tsp salt

1 tsp ground cumin

1 tsp ground turmeric

1 tsp bicarbonate of soda

½ tsp chilli powder

2 tsp lemon juice

2 tbsp vegetable or groundnut oil, plus extra for deep-frying

2–8 tbsp water

2 onions, thinly sliced

2 tsp coriander seeds, lightly crushed

CHEESE PUFFS WITH SALSA

To make the salsa, heat the olive oil in a saucepan. Add the onion and fry for 5 minutes, or until softened but not browned. Add the garlic and fry for a further 30 seconds. Add the wine and allow to bubble, then stir in all the remaining salsa ingredients with salt and pepper to taste and simmer, uncovered, for 10–15 minutes, or until a thick sauce has formed. Spoon into a serving bowl and reserve until ready to serve.

Meanwhile, prepare the cheese puffs. Place the olive oil and water in a saucepan and slowly bring to the boil. As soon as the water boils, remove from the heat and quickly add the flour all at once. Using a wooden spoon, beat the mixture until it is smooth and leaves the sides of the saucepan.

Leave the mixture to cool for 1–2 minutes, then gradually add the eggs, beating hard after each addition and keeping the mixture stiff. Add the cheese and paprika, season to taste with salt and pepper and mix well. Store in the refrigerator until you are ready to fry the cheese puffs.

Just before serving the cheese puffs, heat the sunflower oil in a deep-fat fryer to 180–190°C/350–375°F, or until a cube of bread browns in 30 seconds. Drop teaspoonfuls of the prepared mixture, in batches, into the hot oil and deep-fry for 2–3 minutes, turning once, or until golden brown and crispy. They should rise to the surface of the oil and puff up. Drain well on kitchen paper.

Serve the puffs piping hot, accompanied by the salsa for dipping.

PATATAS BRAVAS

Heat the 2 tablespoons of oil in a saucepan, add the onion and cook over a medium heat, stirring occasionally, for 5 minutes, or until softened but not browned. Add the garlic and cook, stirring, for 30 seconds. Add the wine and bring to the boil. Add the tomatoes, vinegar, chillies and paprika, reduce the heat and simmer, uncovered, for 10–15 minutes until a thick sauce forms.

When the sauce is cooked, use a hand-held blender to blend until smooth. Alternatively, transfer the sauce to a food processor and process until smooth. Return the sauce to the saucepan and set aside.

Do not peel the potatoes, but cut them into chunky pieces. Heat enough oil in a large frying pan to come about 2.5 cm/1 inch up the sides of the pan. Add the potato pieces and cook over a medium–high heat, turning occasionally, for 10–15 minutes until golden brown. Remove with a slotted spoon, drain on kitchen paper and sprinkle with salt to taste.

Meanwhile, gently reheat the sauce. Transfer the potatoes to a warmed serving dish and drizzle over the sauce. Serve hot, with wooden cocktail sticks to spear the potatoes.

Serves 6

2 tbsp Spanish olive oil, plus extra for shallow-frying

1 onion, finely chopped

2 garlic cloves, crushed

50 ml/2 fl oz white wine or dry Spanish sherry

400 g/14 oz canned chopped tomatoes

2 tsp white or red wine vinegar

1–2 tsp crushed dried chillies

2 tsp hot or sweet smoked Spanish paprika

1 kg/2 lb 4 oz potatoes

salt

VEGETARIAN SAMOSAS

Makes 8

1 carrot, diced

200 g/7 oz sweet potato, diced

85 g/3 oz frozen peas

2 tbsp ghee or vegetable oil

1 onion, chopped

1 garlic clove, chopped

2.5-cm/1-inch piece fresh ginger, grated

1 tsp ground turmeric

1 tsp ground cumin

½ tsp chilli powder

½ tsp garam masala

1 tsp lime juice

salt and pepper

Pastry

150 g/5½ oz plain flour, plus extra for dusting

40 g/1½ oz butter, diced

4 tbsp warm milk

vegetable oil, for frying

lime wedges, to serve

Bring a saucepan of water to the boil, add the carrot and cook for 4 minutes. Add the sweet potato and continue to cook for 4 minutes, then add the peas and cook for a further 3 minutes. Drain.

Heat the ghee in a saucepan over a medium heat, add the onion, garlic, ginger, spices and lime juice and cook, stirring, for 3 minutes. Add the drained vegetables and season to taste with salt and pepper. Cook, stirring, for 2 minutes. Remove from the heat and leave to cool for 15 minutes.

To make the pastry, put the flour into a bowl and rub in the butter. Add the milk and mix to form a dough. Knead briefly and divide into 4 pieces. On a lightly floured work surface, form each piece into a ball and roll out into a circle measuring 17 cm/6½ inches in diameter. Halve each circle, divide the filling between them and brush the edges with water, then fold over into triangles and seal the edges.

Heat 2.5 cm/1 inch of oil in a frying pan to 180–190°C/350–375°F, or until a cube of bread browns in 30 seconds. Cook the samosas in batches for 3–4 minutes, or until golden. Drain on kitchen paper and serve hot with lime wedges.

DEVILLED EGGS

Crack the eggs all over and remove the shells. Halve the eggs lengthways, then carefully remove the yolks. Place the yolks in a nylon sieve set over a bowl and rub through, then mash them with a wooden spoon or fork. If necessary, rinse the egg whites under cold running water and dry very carefully.

Place the pimentos on kitchen paper to dry well, then chop them very finely, reserving 32 small strips. Very finely chop half of the olives. Halve the remaining olives and reserve. Add the chopped pimentos and chopped olives to the mashed egg yolks. Add the mayonnaise and mix together well, then add the Tabasco, cayenne and salt and pepper to taste.

Place the egg yolk mixture into a piping bag fitted with a 1-cm/½-inch plain nozzle and pipe the mixture into the hollow in the egg whites. Alternatively, for a simpler finish, use a teaspoon to spoon the prepared filling into each egg half.

Arrange the stuffed egg halves on a serving plate and top each with 2 of the reserved pimento strips and 1 of the reserved olive halves. Dust with a little paprika, garnish with lettuce leaves and serve.

Serves 8

8 large hard-boiled eggs
2 whole canned or bottled pimentos
16 stoned green Spanish olives
5 tbsp mayonnaise
8 drops of Tabasco sauce
large pinch of cayenne pepper
salt and pepper
paprika, for dusting
lettuce leaves, to garnish

SPICY MARINATED OLIVES

Using the flat side of a broad knife, lightly crush each garlic clove. Using a pestle and mortar, crack the coriander seeds. Cut the lemon, with its rind, into small chunks.

Place the olives, garlic, coriander seeds, lemon chunks, thyme sprigs, fennel and chillies in a large bowl and toss together. Season to taste with pepper. (You should not need to add salt as the olives are salty enough.) Pack the ingredients tightly into a sterilized glass jar with a lid. Pour in enough olive oil to cover the olives, then seal the jar tightly.

Leave the olives at room temperature for 24 hours, then place in the refrigerator to marinate for at least 1 week but preferably 2 weeks before serving. From time to time, gently give the jar a shake to re-mix the ingredients. To serve, return the olives to room temperature and remove from the oil.

CHILLI CORNBREAD

Preheat the oven to 180°C/350°F/Gas Mark 4.

Place the polenta, flour and baking powder in a large bowl, then stir in the onion and chillies.

Heat the oil in a 23-cm/9-inch heavy-based frying pan with a heatproof handle, tipping the pan to coat the base and sides with the oil.

Make a well in the centre of the ingredients in the bowl. Add the sweetcorn, soured cream and eggs, then pour in the hot oil from the frying pan. Stir lightly until combined. Pour into the hot pan and smooth the surface.

Bake in the preheated oven for 35–40 minutes, or until a skewer inserted into the centre comes out clean. Cut into wedges and serve warm from the pan.

Serves 8

140 g/5 oz polenta

70 g/2½ oz plain flour

3 tsp baking powder

1 small onion, finely chopped

1–2 fresh green chillies, such as jalapeño, deseeded and chopped

4 tbsp vegetable oil

125 g/4½ oz canned creamed-style sweetcorn

225 ml/8 fl oz soured cream

2 eggs, beaten

SPICY CHICKEN WINGS

Serves 4

900 g/2 lb chicken wings

11 garlic cloves, finely chopped

juice of 2 limes

juice of 1 orange

2 tbsp tequila

1 tbsp mild chilli powder

2 dried chipotle chillies, soaked in hot water for 15 minutes, drained and puréed

2 tbsp vegetable oil

1 tsp sugar

1/4 tsp ground allspice

pinch of ground cinnamon

pinch of ground cumin

pinch of dried oregano

lime wedges, to serve

Cut the chicken wings into 2 pieces at the joint.

Place the chicken wings in a non-metallic dish and add the remaining ingredients. Toss well to coat, then cover and leave to marinate in the refrigerator for at least 3 hours or overnight.

Preheat the barbecue. Cook the chicken wings over hot coals, turning occasionally, for 15–20 minutes, or until crisply browned and the juices run clear when a skewer is inserted into the thickest part of the meat. Alternatively, cook in a ridged griddle pan or under a hot grill. Serve at once with lime wedges for squeezing over.

CHICKEN SATAY SKEWERS WITH PEANUT SAUCE

Put the chicken in a shallow dish. Mix the soy sauce, cornflour, garlic and ginger together in a small bowl and pour over the chicken. Cover and leave to marinate in the refrigerator for at least 2 hours. Meanwhile, soak 12 wooden skewers in cold water for at least 30 minutes.

Preheat the oven to 190°C/375°F/Gas Mark 5. Divide the chicken cubes between the skewers. Heat a ridged griddle pan until hot, add the skewers and cook over a high heat for 3–4 minutes, turning occasionally, until browned all over. Transfer the skewers to a baking tray and cook in the preheated oven for 5–8 minutes, until cooked through.

Meanwhile, to make the sauce, heat the oil in a saucepan, add the onion and garlic and cook over a medium heat, stirring frequently, for 3–4 minutes, until softened. Add the peanut butter, water and chilli powder and simmer for 2–3 minutes, until softened and thinned.

Serve the skewers immediately with the warm sauce and the cucumber.

Serves 4

4 skinless, boneless chicken breasts, about 115 g/4 oz each, cut into 2-cm/¾-inch cubes

4 tbsp soy sauce

1 tbsp cornflour

2 garlic cloves, finely chopped

2.5-cm/1-inch piece fresh ginger, peeled and finely chopped

cucumber cubes, to serve

Peanut sauce

2 tbsp groundnut or vegetable oil

½ onion, finely chopped

1 garlic clove, finely chopped

4 tbsp crunchy peanut butter

4–5 tbsp water

½ tsp chilli powder

BEEF BURGERS WITH CHILLI

Serves 4

Put the beef, red pepper, garlic, chillies, chopped basil and cumin into a bowl and mix until well combined. Season to taste with salt and pepper. Using your hands, form the mixture into 4 equal-sized burgers.

Preheat the barbecue. Cook the burgers over hot coals for 5–8 minutes on each side, or until cooked right through. Alternatively, cook in a ridged griddle pan or under a hot grill. Garnish with basil sprigs and serve in hamburger buns.

CLASSIC BEEF FAJITAS

Combine the beef with the garlic, lime juice, chilli powder, paprika, cumin and olive oil. Add salt and pepper to taste, mix well and leave to marinate for at least 30 minutes at room temperature, or up to overnight in the refrigerator.

To make the salsa, place the tomatoes in a bowl with the spring onions, green chillies, coriander and radishes. Season to taste with cumin, salt and pepper. Reserve.

Warm the tortillas in a lightly greased non-stick frying pan, wrapping each in foil as you work to keep it warm.

Heat the sunflower oil in a large heavy-based frying pan over a high heat. Add the meat and stir-fry until browned and just cooked through.

Divide the sizzling hot beef between the warmed tortillas. Transfer the salsa, chopped avocado and soured cream to individual serving dishes and serve separately for each person to make his or her own fajitas.

Serves 4–6

700 g/1 lb 9 oz beef skirt steak, cut into strips

6 garlic cloves, chopped

juice of 1 lime

large pinch of mild chilli powder

large pinch of paprika

large pinch of ground cumin

1–2 tbsp extra virgin olive oil

12 flour tortillas

1 tbsp vegetable oil, plus extra for greasing

salt and pepper

1–2 avocados, stoned, chopped and tossed in lime juice, to serve

125 ml/4 fl oz soured cream, to serve

Pico de gallo salsa

8 ripe tomatoes, diced

3 spring onions, sliced

1–2 fresh green chillies, such as jalapeño or serrano, deseeded and chopped

3–4 tbsp chopped fresh coriander

5–8 radishes, diced

ground cumin

salt and pepper

Serves 6

Spanish olive oil, for greasing

1.25 kg/2 lb 12 oz pork spare ribs

100 ml/3½ fl oz dry Spanish sherry

5 tsp hot or sweet smoked Spanish paprika

2 garlic cloves, crushed

1 tbsp dried oregano

150 ml/5 fl oz water

salt

SPARE RIBS WITH PAPRIKA SAUCE

Preheat the oven to 220°C/425°F/Gas Mark 7. Grease a large roasting tin.

If the butcher has not already done so, cut the sheets of spare ribs into individual ribs. If possible, cut each spare rib in half widthways. Put the spare ribs in the prepared tin, in a single layer, and roast in the preheated oven for 20 minutes.

Meanwhile, make the sauce. Put the sherry, paprika, garlic, oregano, water and salt to taste in a jug and mix together well.

Reduce the oven temperature to 180°C/350°F/Gas Mark 4. Pour off the fat from the tin, then pour the sauce over the spare ribs and turn the spare ribs to coat with the sauce. Roast for a further 45 minutes, until tender, basting the spare ribs with the sauce once halfway through the cooking time.

Pile the spare ribs into a warmed serving dish. Place the roasting tin over a high heat on the hob and bring the sauce to the boil, then reduce the heat and simmer until reduced by half. Pour the sauce over the spare ribs and serve hot.

CHORIZO &
MUSHROOM KEBABS

Heat the oil in a frying pan over a medium heat. Add the chorizo and fry for 20 seconds, stirring.

Add the mushrooms and continue frying for a further 1–2 minutes, until the mushrooms begin to brown and absorb the fat in the frying pan.

Thread a green pepper square, a piece of chorizo and a mushroom onto a cocktail stick. Continue until all the ingredients are used. Serve hot or at room temperature.

Serves 8

2 tbsp Spanish olive oil

24 slices chorizo, each about 1 cm/½ inch thick (about 100 g/3½ oz)

24 button mushrooms, wiped

1 green pepper, grilled, peeled and cut into 24 squares

BARBECUED CAJUN PORK BURGERS

Cook the sweet potato in a saucepan of lightly salted boiling water for 15–20 minutes, or until soft when pierced with a fork. Drain well, then mash and reserve.

Place the pork in a bowl, add the mashed potato, apple and Cajun seasoning. Grate 1 of the onions and add to the pork mixture with the coriander and salt and pepper to taste. Mix together, then shape into 4–6 equal-sized burgers. Cover and leave to chill in the refrigerator for 1 hour.

Slice the remaining onions. Heat 1 tablespoon of the oil in a frying pan. Add the onions and cook over a low heat for 10–12 minutes, stirring until soft. Remove the frying pan from the heat and reserve. Wrap each burger in 2 bacon rashers.

Preheat the barbecue. Cook the burgers over hot coals, brushing with the remaining oil, for 4–5 minutes on each side, or until thoroughly cooked. Alternatively, cook in a ridged griddle pan or under a hot grill. Serve with the fried onions.

CRAB, PORK & CHILLI FRITTERS

Put all the fritter ingredients, except the oil, in a food processor and process to a coarse paste. Use damp hands to shape into 20 small, flat cakes.

Heat enough oil to cover the base of a large frying pan, add the fritters, in 2–3 batches, and cook over a medium–high heat for 2 minutes on each side, or until browned and cooked through. Remove with a slotted spoon, drain on kitchen paper and keep warm while you cook the remaining fritters.

To make the dipping sauce, put the water, sugar and vinegar in a small saucepan and heat gently until the sugar has dissolved. Add the onion and cucumber and simmer for 5 minutes. Serve warm, or cold, in a small serving dish with the fritters.

Serves 4

Fritters

115 g/4 oz canned white crabmeat, drained

115 g/4 oz fresh pork mince

2 fresh red chillies, deseeded and roughly chopped

1 tsp salt

2 spring onions, chopped

handful of fresh coriander, chopped

1 egg white

groundnut or vegetable oil, for shallow-frying

Dipping sauce

150 ml/5 fl oz water

4 tbsp caster sugar

1 tbsp rice vinegar

½ small red onion, very finely diced

5-cm/2-inch piece cucumber, very finely diced

FISH TIKKA

Makes 8

pinch of saffron threads, pounded

1 tbsp hot milk

85 g/3 oz Greek-style yogurt

1 tbsp garlic purée

1 tbsp ginger purée

1 tsp salt, or to taste

½ tsp granulated sugar

juice of ½ lemon

½–1 tsp chilli powder

½ tsp garam masala

1 tsp ground fennel seeds

2 tsp gram flour

750 g/1 lb 10 oz salmon fillets, skinned and cut into 5-cm/ 2-inch cubes

3 tbsp olive oil, plus extra for brushing

sliced tomatoes and cucumber, to garnish

lemon wedges, to serve

Soak the pounded saffron in the hot milk for 10 minutes.

Put all the remaining ingredients, except the fish and oil, in a bowl and beat with a fork or a wire whisk until smooth. Stir in the saffron and milk, mix well and add the fish cubes. Using a metal spoon, mix gently, turning the fish around until fully coated with the marinade. Cover and leave to marinate in the refrigerator for 2 hours. Return to room temperature before cooking.

Preheat the grill to high. Brush the rack generously with oil and 8 metal skewers lightly with oil. Line the grill pan with a piece of foil.

Thread the fish cubes onto the prepared skewers, leaving a narrow gap between each piece. Arrange on the prepared rack and cook about 10 cm/4 inches below the heat source for 3 minutes. Brush half the 3 tablespoons of oil over the kebabs and cook for a further minute. Turn over and brush any remaining marinade over the fish. Cook for 3 minutes. Brush the remaining oil over the fish and cook for a further 2 minutes, or until the fish is lightly charred.

Remove from the heat and leave to rest for 5 minutes. Serve garnished with the tomatoes and cucumber and with lemon wedges for squeezing over.

FISH BURRITOS

Season the fish to taste with salt and pepper, then place in a pan with the cumin, oregano, garlic, and enough stock to cover.

Bring to the boil, then cook for 1 minute. Remove the pan from the heat. Let the fish cool in the cooking liquid for 30 minutes.

Remove the fish from the liquid with a slotted spoon and break up into bite-sized pieces. Place in a non-metallic bowl, sprinkle with the lemon juice and set aside.

Heat the tortillas, one at a time, in a non-stick frying pan, sprinkling them with a few drops of water as they heat. Wrap each tortilla in foil or a clean tea towel to keep it warm while you heat up the rest.

Arrange a little shredded lettuce in the centre of each tortilla, spoon on a few big chunks of the fish, then sprinkle with the tomatoes and roll up. Spoon over some salsa and repeat with the other tortillas. Serve immediately, garnished with lemon wedges.

Makes 8

450 g/1 lb firm-fleshed white fish, such as red snapper or cod

¼ tsp ground cumin

pinch of dried oregano

4 garlic cloves, very finely chopped

about 150 ml/5 fl oz fish stock

juice of ½ lemon or lime

8 flour tortillas

2–3 romaine lettuce leaves, shredded

2 ripe tomatoes, diced

salt and pepper

salsa, to serve

lemon wedges, to garnish

SIZZLING CHILLI PRAWNS

Pull the heads off the prawns and peel, leaving the tails intact. Cut along the length of the back of each prawn and remove and discard the dark vein. Rinse the prawns under cold running water and pat dry on kitchen paper.

Cut the chilli in half lengthways, remove the seeds and finely chop the flesh.

Heat the oil in a large heavy-based frying pan or flameproof casserole until quite hot, then add the garlic and fry for 30 seconds. Add the prawns, chilli, paprika and salt and fry for 2–3 minutes, stirring constantly, until the prawns turn pink and begin to curl.

Serve the prawns in the cooking dish, still sizzling. Accompany with wooden cocktail sticks, to spear the prawns, and serve with crusty bread to mop up the aromatic cooking oil.

PRAWN REMOULADE

To make the sauce, put the spring onions, celery, garlic and parsley into a food processor and pulse until finely chopped. Add the mustard, sugar, vinegar, horseradish, paprika, cayenne pepper, salt, pepper and hot pepper sauce to taste and whizz until well blended. With the motor running, pour in the oil through the feed tube in a slow, steady stream until a thick, creamy sauce forms. Transfer to a large bowl, cover and reserve.

Put the salt and lemon slices in a large saucepan of water and bring to the boil over a high heat. Reduce the heat so that the water simmers gently. Add the prawns and cook for 3–5 minutes, or until they turn pink.

Drain the prawns well and rinse them under cold water until cooled. Peel and devein them, adding them to the sauce as you go. Stir together, then cover and leave to chill for at least 45 minutes, but ideally overnight. Serve on a bed of lettuce with hard-boiled eggs and sliced tomatoes.

Serves 4–6

1½ tbsp salt

1 lemon, sliced

800 g/1 lb 12 oz large unpeeled raw prawns

shredded iceberg lettuce, hard-boiled eggs and sliced tomatoes, to serve

Remoulade sauce

55 g/2 oz spring onions, roughly chopped

55 g/2 oz celery sticks, roughly chopped

1 large garlic clove

4 tbsp chopped fresh parsley

2 tbsp Creole mustard

2 tbsp caster sugar

2 tbsp cider vinegar or tomato ketchup

1½ tbsp prepared horseradish

1 tbsp paprika

½ tsp cayenne pepper

½ tsp salt

¼ tsp ground black pepper

hot pepper sauce, to taste

about 150 ml/5 fl oz groundnut oil

LAKSA

Serves 4

1 tbsp sunflower oil

2–3 garlic cloves, cut into thin slivers

1–2 fresh red Thai chillies, deseeded and sliced

2 lemon grass stalks, outer leaves removed, chopped

2.5-cm/1-inch piece fresh ginger, grated

1.2 litres/2 pints fish or vegetable stock

350 g/12 oz large raw prawns, peeled and deveined

115 g/4 oz shiitake mushrooms, sliced

1 large carrot, grated

55 g/2 oz dried egg noodles (optional)

1–2 tsp Thai fish sauce

1 tbsp chopped fresh coriander

Heat the oil in a large saucepan over a medium heat, add the garlic, chillies, lemon grass and ginger and cook for 5 minutes, stirring frequently. Add the stock and bring to the boil, then reduce the heat and simmer for 5 minutes.

Stir in the prawns, mushrooms and carrot. Break the noodles, if using, into short lengths, add to the saucepan and simmer for a further 5 minutes, or until the prawns have turned pink and the noodles are tender.

Stir in the Thai fish sauce and coriander and heat through for a further minute before serving.

HOT & SOUR SOUP

Mix the chillies and vinegar together in a non-metallic bowl, cover and leave to stand at room temperature for 1 hour.

Meanwhile, bring the stock to the boil in a saucepan. Add the lemon grass, soy sauce, sugar and lime juice, reduce the heat and simmer for 20–30 minutes.

Heat the oil in a preheated wok, add the tofu cubes and stir-fry over a high heat for 2–3 minutes, or until browned all over. (You may need to do this in 2 batches, depending on the size of the wok.) Remove with a slotted spoon and drain on kitchen paper.

Add the chillies and vinegar with the tofu, mushrooms and half the spring onions to the stock mixture and cook for 10 minutes. Mix the remaining spring onions with the pak choi and scatter over the soup before serving.

Serves 4

2 fresh red chillies, deseeded and roughly chopped

6 tbsp rice vinegar

1.2 litres/2 pints vegetable stock

2 lemon grass stalks, halved

4 tbsp soy sauce

1 tbsp palm sugar

juice of ½ lime

2 tbsp groundnut or vegetable oil

225 g/8 oz firm tofu (drained weight), cut into 1-cm/½-inch cubes

400 g/14 oz canned straw mushrooms, drained

4 spring onions, chopped

1 small head of pak choi, shredded

SPICY RED LENTIL SOUP

Put the lentils and stock into a large saucepan with a tight-fitting lid. Place over a high heat and slowly bring to the boil, skimming the surface as necessary. Add the chillies and turmeric, reduce the heat to very low, cover the pan and leave the lentils to simmer for 25–30 minutes, until they are very soft and mushy.

Meanwhile, heat the oil in a separate large saucepan over a medium heat. Add the onions and garlic and fry for 5–7 minutes, until the onions are tender but not brown. Add the curry paste and cook, stirring, for about a minute.

Tip the lentils and any remaining water into the pan with the onion mixture and stir together.

Put the mixture into a blender or food processor and whizz until blended. Return the mixture to the rinsed-out pan and add enough water to make a thin soup. Slowly bring to the boil. Reduce the heat, season to taste with salt and pepper and simmer for 2 minutes.

Ladle into warmed soup bowls, swirl in a spoonful of yogurt and sprinkle with coriander. Serve with the warmed naan breads.

BLAZING

Meat & poultry mains

TEQUILA-MARINATED BEEF STEAKS

Place the oil, tequila, orange and lime juices, garlic, chilli powder, cumin, oregano and salt and pepper to taste in a large, shallow non-metallic dish and mix together. Add the steaks and turn to coat in the marinade. Cover and chill in the refrigerator for at least 2 hours or overnight, turning occasionally.

Preheat the barbecue and oil the rack. Let the steaks return to room temperature, then remove from the marinade. Cook over hot coals for 3–4 minutes on each side for medium, or longer according to taste, basting frequently with the marinade. Alternatively, cook in a ridged griddle pan or under a hot grill. Serve at once.

Serves 4

2 tbsp olive oil, plus extra for brushing

3 tbsp tequila

3 tbsp freshly squeezed orange juice

1 tbsp freshly squeezed lime juice

3 garlic cloves, crushed

2 tsp chilli powder

2 tsp ground cumin

1 tsp dried oregano

4 sirloin steaks

salt and pepper

CHILLI CON CARNE

Serves 6

4 tbsp sunflower oil

2 onions, chopped

1 garlic clove, chopped

1 tbsp plain flour

900 g/2 lb stewing steak, diced

300 ml/10 fl oz beef stock

300 ml/10 fl oz red wine

2–3 fresh red chillies, deseeded and chopped

800 g/1 lb 12 oz canned red kidney beans, drained and rinsed

400 g/14 oz canned chopped tomatoes

salt and pepper

tortilla chips, to serve

Heat half of the oil in a heavy-based saucepan. Add half the chopped onion and the garlic and cook, stirring occasionally, for 5 minutes, until softened. Remove with a slotted spoon.

Place the flour on a plate and season well with salt and pepper, then toss the meat in the flour to coat. Cook the meat, in batches, until browned all over, then return the meat and the onion mixture to the saucepan. Pour in the stock and wine and bring to the boil, stirring. Reduce the heat and simmer for 1 hour.

Meanwhile, heat the remaining oil in a frying pan. Add the remaining onion and the chillies and cook, stirring occasionally, for 5 minutes. Add the beans and tomatoes with their juice and break up with a wooden spoon. Simmer for 25 minutes, until thickened.

Divide the meat between individual plates, top with the bean mixture and serve with tortilla chips.

67

BEEF GOULASH

Heat the oil in a large frying pan and cook the onion and garlic for 3–4 minutes.

Cut the stewing steak into chunks and cook over a high heat for 3 minutes, until browned all over. Add the paprika and stir well, then add the tomatoes, tomato purée, red pepper and mushrooms. Cook for 2 minutes, stirring frequently.

Pour in the beef stock. Bring to the boil, then reduce the heat. Cover and simmer for 1½–2 hours, until the meat is tender.

Blend the cornflour with the water in a small bowl, then add to the pan, stirring until thickened and smooth. Cook for 1 minute, then season to taste with salt and pepper.

Transfer the beef goulash to a warmed serving dish, garnish with chopped fresh parsley and serve with rice.

Serves 4

2 tbsp vegetable oil

1 large onion, chopped

1 garlic clove, crushed

750 g/1 lb 10 oz lean stewing steak

2 tbsp paprika

425 g/15 oz canned chopped tomatoes

2 tbsp tomato purée

1 large red pepper, deseeded and chopped

175 g/6 oz mushrooms, sliced

600 ml/1 pint beef stock

1 tbsp cornflour

1 tbsp water

salt and pepper

chopped fresh parsley, to garnish

cooked long-grain and wild rice, to serve

PEPPER POT STEW

Trim any fat or gristle from the beef and cut into 2.5-cm/ 1-inch chunks. Toss the beef in the flour until well coated and reserve any remaining flour.

Heat the oil in a large heavy-based saucepan and cook the onion, garlic, chilli and celery with the cloves and allspice, stirring frequently, for 5 minutes, or until softened. Add the beef and cook over a high heat, stirring frequently, for 3 minutes, or until browned on all sides and sealed. Sprinkle in the reserved flour and cook, stirring constantly, for 2 minutes, then remove from the heat.

Add the hot pepper sauce and gradually stir in the stock, then return to the heat and bring to the boil, stirring. Reduce the heat, cover and simmer, stirring occasionally, for 1½ hours.

Add the squash and red pepper to the saucepan and simmer for a further 15 minutes. Add the tomatoes and okra and simmer for a further 15 minutes, or until the beef is tender. Serve at once.

Serves 4

STIR-FRIED BEEF WITH CHILLI RICE

To make the chilli rice, heat the oil in a preheated wok, add the spring onions, green beans and chillies and stir-fry over a medium–high heat for 1–2 minutes. Add the rice and stir-fry for 2–3 minutes. Add the stock and bring to the boil, stirring occasionally. Reduce the heat and simmer gently for 10–15 minutes, until the rice is tender, adding more stock if necessary. Remove from the heat but keep the rice warm in the wok.

To make the stir-fried beef, heat the oil in a separate preheated wok or large frying pan, add the onion, green pepper and ginger and stir-fry over a medium–high heat for 30 seconds. Add the beef and stir-fry over a high heat for 1–2 minutes, until browned all over. Add the oyster sauce, soy sauce and sugar and stir-fry for 2–3 minutes, until heated through. Serve the stir-fried beef immediately with the chilli rice, garnished with coriander.

Serves 4

Chilli rice

2 tbsp groundnut or vegetable oil

5 spring onions, chopped

55 g/2 oz fine green beans, trimmed and halved

2 fresh red chillies, deseeded and sliced

225 g/8 oz basmati rice

about 600 ml/1 pint beef stock

Stir-fried beef

2 tbsp groundnut or vegetable oil

1 onion, cut into wedges

1 green pepper, deseeded and cut into chunks

2.5-cm/1-inch piece fresh ginger, finely chopped

350 g/12 oz beef fillet, cut into strips

6 tbsp oyster sauce

2 tbsp soy sauce

1 tsp palm sugar

chopped fresh coriander, to garnish

BEEF MADRAS

Depending on how hot you want this dish to be, chop the chillies with or without any seeds. The more seeds you include, the hotter the dish will be. Put the chopped chilli and any seeds in a small bowl with the coriander, turmeric, mustard seeds, ginger and pepper and stir in a little of the dissolved creamed coconut to make a thin paste.

Melt the ghee in a flameproof casserole or large frying pan with a tight fitting lid over a medium-high heat. Add the onions and garlic and cook for 5–8 minutes, stirring frequently, until the onions are golden brown. Add the spice paste and stir around for 2 minutes, or until you can smell the aromas.

Add the meat and stock and bring to the boil. Reduce the heat to its lowest level, cover tightly and simmer for 1½ hours, or until the beef is tender. Check occasionally that the meat isn't catching on the base of the pan and stir in a little extra water or stock, if necessary.

Uncover the pan and stir in the remaining dissolved coconut cream with the lemon juice and salt to taste. Bring to the boil, stirring, then reduce the heat again and simmer, still uncovered, until the sauce reduces slightly. Serve with poppadoms.

Serves 4–6

1–2 dried red chillies

2 tsp ground coriander

2 tsp ground turmeric

1 tsp black mustard seeds

½ tsp ground ginger

¼ tsp pepper

140 g/5 oz creamed coconut, grated, dissolved in 300 ml/ 10 fl oz boiling water

55 g/2 oz ghee or 4 tbsp vegetable or groundnut oil

2 onions, chopped

3 large garlic cloves, chopped

700 g/1 lb 9 oz lean stewing steak, such as chuck, trimmed and cut into 5-cm/2-inch cubes

250 ml/9 fl oz beef stock

lemon juice

salt

poppadoms, to serve

TAGINE OF LAMB

Heat the oil in a large heavy-based frying pan or flameproof casserole over a medium heat. Add the onion and lamb and cook, stirring frequently, for 5 minutes, or until the meat is lightly browned all over. Add the garlic, stock, orange rind and juice, honey, cinnamon stick and ginger. Bring to the boil, then reduce the heat, cover and leave to simmer for 45 minutes.

Using a sharp knife, halve the aubergine lengthways and slice thinly. Add to the frying pan with the tomatoes and apricots. Cover and cook for a further 45 minutes, or until the lamb is tender.

Stir in the coriander and season to taste with salt and pepper. Transfer to a warmed serving dish and serve with couscous.

Serves 4

1 tbsp sunflower oil

1 onion, chopped

350 g/12 oz boneless lamb, trimmed of all visible fat and cut into 2.5-cm/1-inch cubes

1 garlic clove, finely chopped

600 ml/1 pint vegetable stock

grated rind and juice of 1 orange

1 tsp clear honey

1 cinnamon stick

1-cm/½-inch piece fresh ginger, finely chopped

1 aubergine

4 tomatoes, peeled and chopped

115 g/4 oz ready-to-eat dried apricots

2 tbsp chopped fresh coriander

salt and pepper

cooked couscous, to serve

TURKISH LAMB CASSEROLE

Serves 4

2 tbsp olive oil

[ingredients list — largely illegible]

Preheat the oven to 160°C/325°F/Gas Mark 3. Heat half the oil in a large non-stick frying pan over a high heat, add the lamb shanks and cook, turning frequently, for 2–3 minutes, until browned all over. Transfer to a casserole.

Heat the remaining oil in the frying pan over a medium–high heat, add the onions and peppers and cook, stirring frequently, for 10–15 minutes, or until the onions are softened and just turning golden. Add the garlic, aubergine and spices and cook, stirring constantly, for 1 minute. Add the chickpeas, tomatoes and their juice, herbs and enough stock to cover the base of the frying pan by about 2 cm/¾ inch, stir well and bring to a simmer. Season to taste with salt and pepper and transfer to a casserole.

Cover the casserole, transfer to the middle shelf of the preheated oven and cook for 1½ hours. Check after 45 minutes that the casserole is gently bubbling and that there is enough liquid – if it looks rather dry, add a little more stock or boiling water. Serve with couscous.

LAMB ROGAN JOSH

Heat half of the ghee in a large saucepan over a high heat. Add the lamb and cook, stirring, for 5 minutes. Lift out the meat with a slotted spoon and drain on kitchen paper. Set aside.

Add the garlic, chillies, ginger, poppy seeds and ground spices to the saucepan and cook over a medium heat, stirring, for 4 minutes. Remove from the heat, leave to cool for a few minutes, then transfer the spice mixture to a food processor. Stir in the soured cream, turmeric and chilli powder and process the mixture until smooth.

Heat the remaining ghee in the rinsed-out saucepan over a low heat. Add the tomatoes and cook, stirring, for 3 minutes. Add the soured cream mixture and cook, stirring, until the oil separates. Remove from the heat and add the reserved lamb. Add the bay leaf, return the saucepan to the heat and cover. Simmer gently for 35–40 minutes, or until most of the liquid has been absorbed. Remove from the heat and discard the bay leaf.

Garnish with coriander leaves and serve with rice.

Serves 4

125 ml/4 fl oz ghee or vegetable oil

500 g/1 lb 2 oz boneless lamb, cut into bite-sized chunks

4 garlic cloves, chopped

3 fresh green chillies, chopped

2.5-cm/1-inch piece fresh ginger, grated

1 tsp poppy seeds

1 cinnamon stick, ground

1 cardamom pod, ground

4 cloves, ground

1 tsp coriander seeds, ground

1 tsp cumin seeds, ground

250 ml/9 fl oz soured cream

½ tsp ground turmeric

½ tsp chilli powder

2 large tomatoes, chopped

1 bay leaf

fresh coriander leaves, to garnish

cooked rice, to serve

LAMB & SPINACH CURRY

Serves 2–4

300 ml/10 fl oz vegetable oil

2 onions, sliced

¼ bunch of fresh coriander, chopped

2 fresh green chillies, chopped

1½ tsp finely chopped fresh ginger

1½ tsp crushed fresh garlic

1 tsp chilli powder

½ tsp ground turmeric

450 g/1 lb lean lamb, cut into bite-sized chunks

1 tsp salt

1 kg/2 lb 4 oz fresh spinach, trimmed, washed and chopped

700 ml/1¼ pints water

finely chopped fresh red chilli, to garnish

Heat the oil in a large heavy-based frying pan. Add the onions and cook until light golden.

Add the coriander and green chillies to the frying pan and stir-fry for 3–5 minutes. Reduce the heat and add the ginger, garlic, chilli powder and turmeric, stirring well.

Add the lamb to the frying pan and stir-fry for a further 5 minutes. Add the salt and the spinach and cook, stirring occasionally with a wooden spoon, for a further 3–5 minutes.

Add the water, stirring, and cook over a low heat, covered, for 45 minutes. Remove the lid and check the meat. If it is not tender, turn the meat over, increase the heat and cook, uncovered, until the surplus water has been absorbed. Stir-fry the mixture for a further 5–7 minutes.

Transfer the lamb and spinach mixture to a serving dish and garnish with chopped red chilli. Serve hot.

83

MARINATED LAMB BROCHETTES

Put the meat in a large non-metallic bowl and add the vinegar, salt and garlic and ginger purées. Mix together thoroughly, cover and leave to marinate in the refrigerator for 30 minutes.

Put the yogurt and gram flour in a separate bowl and beat together with a fork until smooth. Add the cumin, garam masala, chilli powder, turmeric and oil and mix together thoroughly. Add the yogurt mixture to the marinated meat, then add the peppers and shallots and stir until well blended. Cover and leave to marinate in the refrigerator for 2–3 hours, or overnight. Return to room temperature before cooking.

Preheat the grill to high. Line the grill pan with a piece of foil. Brush the rack and 4 metal skewers with the oil.

Thread the marinated lamb, peppers and shallots alternately onto the prepared skewers. Place the skewers on the prepared rack and cook under the preheated grill for 4 minutes. Brush generously with half the melted butter and cook for a further 2 minutes. Turn over and cook for 3–4 minutes. Brush with the remaining butter and cook for a further 2 minutes.

Balance the brochettes over a large saucepan or frying pan and leave to rest for 5–6 minutes before sliding off the skewers with a knife. Serve with the lemon wedges.

Serves 4

700 g/1 lb 9 oz boned leg of lamb, cut into 2.5-cm/1-inch cubes

2 tbsp light malt vinegar

½ tsp salt, or to taste

1 tbsp garlic purée

1 tbsp ginger purée

115 g/4 oz whole milk natural yogurt, strained, or Greek-style yogurt

1 tbsp gram flour

1 tsp ground cumin

1 tsp garam masala

½–1 tsp chilli powder

½ tsp ground turmeric

3 tbsp olive or sunflower oil, plus 1 tbsp for brushing

½ red pepper, deseeded and cut into 2.5-cm/1-inch pieces

½ green pepper, deseeded and cut into 2.5-cm/1-inch pieces

8 shallots, halved

55 g/2 oz butter, melted

lemon wedges, to serve

PORK VINDALOO

Serves 4

6 whole dried red chillies
5 cloves
1/4 tsp almond slices
4 black cardamom pods
1/2 tsp black peppercorns
1g mace blade
1/2 tsp nutmeg, finely grated
1 tbsp cumin seeds
1/2 tsp coriander seeds
1 tsp fennel seeds
2 tbsp garlic purée
1 tbsp ginger purée
120ml cider vinegar
50ml tamarind juice
juice of 1 lime
900g/1 lb 2 oz boneless leg of pork, diced
4 tbsp sunflower or olive oil
2 large onions, finely chopped
350ml/10 fl oz warm water
1 tsp salt, or to taste
1 tsp soft dark brown sugar
6 large garlic cloves, sliced
8–10 fresh/dried curry leaves

Grind the first 10 ingredients (all the spices) to a fine powder in a spice grinder. Transfer the ground spices to a bowl and add the garlic and ginger purées, vinegar and tamarind juice. Mix together to form a paste.

Put the pork in a large non-metallic bowl and rub about one quarter of the spice paste into the meat. Cover and leave to marinate in the refrigerator for 30–40 minutes.

Heat the 4 tablespoons of the oil in a medium heavy-based saucepan over a medium heat, add the onions and cook, stirring frequently, for 8–10 minutes, until lightly browned. Add the remaining spice paste and cook, stirring constantly, for 5–6 minutes. Add 2 tablespoons of the warm water and cook until it evaporates. Repeat with another 2 tablespoons of warm water.

Add the marinated pork and cook over medium–high heat for 5–6 minutes, until the meat changes colour. Add the salt, sugar and the remaining warm water. Bring to the boil, then reduce the heat to low, cover and simmer for 50–55 minutes.

Meanwhile, heat the remaining oil in a small saucepan over a low heat. Add the sliced garlic and cook, stirring, until it begins to brown. Add the curry leaves and leave to sizzle for 15–20 seconds. Stir the garlic mixture into the vindaloo. Serve immediately.

BURMESE PORK CURRY

Mix the meat, wine and salt in a non-metallic bowl and set aside for 1 hour.

Put the garlic, ginger, chillies and onion in a food processor or blender and blend until the ingredients are mushy. Transfer to a bowl and stir in the turmeric and chilli powder.

Heat both types of oil in a medium heavy-based saucepan over a medium heat and add the puréed ingredients. Stir and cook for 5–6 minutes, reduce the heat to low and continue to cook for a further 8–10 minutes, sprinkling over a little water from time to time to prevent the spices from sticking to the base of the pan.

Add the marinated pork, increase the heat to medium–high and stir until the meat changes colour. Pour in the warm water, bring to the boil, reduce the heat to low, cover and cook for 1 hour 10 minutes, stirring several times during the last 15–20 minutes to prevent the thickened sauce from sticking. Remove from the heat and garnish with the strips of chilli. Serve with basmati rice.

Serves 4

700 g/1 lb 9 oz boneless leg of pork, fat trimmed and cut into 2.5-cm/1-inch cubes

2 tbsp dry white wine

1 tsp salt, or to taste

8 large garlic cloves, roughly chopped

5-cm/2-inch piece fresh ginger, roughly chopped

2 fresh red chillies, roughly chopped

1 large onion, roughly chopped

1 tsp ground turmeric

½–1 tsp chilli powder

3 tbsp groundnut oil

1 tbsp sesame oil

200 ml/7 fl oz warm water

1 fresh green chilli, deseeded and cut into julienne strips, to garnish

cooked basmati rice, to serve

PAD THAI

Serves 4

225 g/8 oz thick dried rice noodles

2 tbsp groundnut or vegetable oil

4 spring onions, roughly chopped

2 garlic cloves, crushed

2 fresh red chillies, deseeded and sliced

225 g/8 oz pork fillet, trimmed and thinly sliced

115 g/4 oz cooked peeled large prawns

juice of 1 lime

2 tbsp Thai fish sauce

2 eggs, beaten

55 g/2 oz fresh beansprouts

handful of fresh coriander, chopped

55 g/2 oz unsalted peanuts, chopped

Soak the noodles in a large saucepan of boiling water, covered, for 10 minutes or according to the packet instructions, until just tender. Drain, rinse under cold running water and set aside.

Heat the oil in a preheated wok, add the spring onions, garlic and chillies and stir-fry over a medium–high heat for 1–2 minutes. Add the pork and stir-fry over a high heat for 1–2 minutes, until browned all over.

Add the prawns, lime juice, fish sauce and eggs and stir-fry over a medium heat for 2–3 minutes, until the eggs have set and the prawns are heated through.

Add the beansprouts, most of the coriander, the peanuts and the reserved noodles and stir-fry for 30 seconds, until heated through. Serve immediately, garnished with the remaining coriander.

RED ROASTED PORK WITH PEPPERED NOODLES

Mix the curry paste and soy sauce together in a small bowl and spread over the pork fillet. Cover and leave to marinate in the refrigerator for 1 hour.

Preheat the oven to 200°C/400°F/Gas Mark 6. Roast the pork in the preheated oven for 20–25 minutes, until cooked through. Remove from the oven, cover with foil and leave to rest for 15 minutes.

Meanwhile, cook the noodles in a large saucepan of boiling water for 4 minutes, or according to the packet instructions, until just tender. Drain, rinse under cold running water and set aside.

Heat the oil in a preheated wok, add the onion, ginger and garlic and stir-fry over a medium–high heat for 1–2 minutes. Add the orange and red peppers and pepper and stir-fry for 2–3 minutes, until tender. Stir in the chives and most of the coriander.

Add the drained noodles to the pepper mixture and toss together until well mixed. Divide between 2 serving dishes. Slice the pork and arrange on top of the noodles. Scatter with the remaining coriander and serve immediately.

Serves 2

1 tbsp Thai red curry paste

2 tbsp soy sauce

350 g/12 oz pork fillet, trimmed

225 g/8 oz fine dried egg noodles

2 tbsp groundnut or vegetable oil

1 red onion, chopped

2.5-cm/1-inch piece fresh ginger, finely chopped

1 garlic clove, finely chopped

1 orange pepper, deseeded and chopped

1 red pepper, deseeded and chopped

1 tbsp pepper

1 small bunch of fresh chives, snipped

handful of fresh coriander, chopped

Serves 4

650 g/1 lb 7 oz skinless chicken breasts

juice of 1 lemon

1 tsp salt

5 tbsp sunflower or olive oil

1 large onion, finely chopped

1 tsp garlic purée

1 tsp ginger purée

½ tsp ground turmeric

1 tsp ground cumin

1 tsp ground coriander

½–1 tsp chilli powder

400 g/14 oz canned chopped tomatoes

150 ml/5 fl oz warm water

1 large garlic clove, chopped

1 small onion, finely chopped

1 small red pepper and ½ small green pepper, deseeded and cut into 2.5-cm/1-inch pieces

1 small onion, cut into thin wedges

1 tsp garam masala

Indian bread or plain boiled basmati rice, to serve

CHICKEN JALFREZI

Cut the chicken into 2.5-cm/1-inch cubes and put in a non-metallic bowl. Add the lemon juice and salt and rub well into the chicken. Cover and leave to marinate in the refrigerator for 20 minutes.

Heat 4 tablespoons of the oil in a medium heavy-based saucepan over a medium heat. Add the onion and cook, stirring frequently, for 8–9 minutes, until lightly browned. Add the garlic and ginger pureés and cook, stirring, for 3 minutes. Add the turmeric, cumin, coriander and chilli powder and cook, stirring, for 1 minute. Add the tomatoes and cook for 2–3 minutes, stirring frequently, until the oil separates from the spice paste.

Add the marinated chicken, increase the heat slightly and cook, stirring, until it changes colour. Add the warm water and bring to the boil. Reduce the heat, cover and simmer for 25 minutes.

Heat the remaining 1 tablespoon of oil in a small saucepan or frying pan over a low heat. Add the garlic and cook, stirring frequently, until browned. Add the red and green peppers, increase the heat to medium and stir-fry for 2 minutes, then stir in the garam masala. Fold the pepper mixture into the curry. Remove from the heat and serve immediately with Indian bread or basmati rice.

CHICKEN WITH APRICOTS & CHICKPEAS

Heat the oil in a flameproof casserole over a medium–high heat. Add the chicken, in batches if necessary, and fry for 3–5 minutes on each side, until golden brown. Remove from the casserole and set aside.

Pour off all but 2 tablespoons of the oil from the casserole. Add the onions and stir for 4 minutes. Add the garlic and continue stirring for 1–2 minutes, until the onions are softened but not browned. Stir in the coriander, ginger, cumin and chilli flakes, if using, and cook, stirring, for 1 minute.

Return the chicken pieces to the casserole with enough water to cover. Bring to the boil, then reduce the heat and leave to simmer for 20 minutes. Add the apricots, chickpeas and saffron and continue to simmer for 10 minutes, or until the chicken pieces are cooked through and the juices run clear.

Transfer the chicken, apricots and chickpeas to a serving platter and keep warm. Bring the liquid remaining in the casserole to the boil and reduce by half. Pour this liquid over the chicken, add the preserved lemon and sprinkle with the flaked almonds. Transfer to serving plates, garnish with parsley sprigs and serve hot, accompanied by couscous.

Serves 4

2 tbsp olive or sunflower oil

1 large chicken, cut into 8 pieces, or 8 chicken thighs

2 large onions, sliced

2 large garlic cloves, crushed

2 tsp ground coriander

1½ tsp ground ginger

1½ tsp ground cumin

pinch of dried chilli flakes, to taste (optional)

400 g/14 oz dried apricots, soaked overnight in 300 ml/ 10 fl oz orange juice

400 g/14 oz canned chickpeas, drained and rinsed

large pinch of saffron threads

1 preserved lemon, rinsed and sliced

30 g/1 oz toasted flaked almonds

fresh flat-leaf parsley sprigs, to garnish

cooked couscous, to serve

THAI GREEN CHICKEN CURRY

Serves 4

2 tbsp groundnut or sunflower oil

2 tbsp Thai green curry paste

500 g/1 lb 2 oz skinless, boneless chicken breasts, cut into cubes

2 kaffir lime leaves, roughly torn

1 lemon grass stalk, finely chopped

225 ml/8 fl oz coconut milk

16 baby aubergines, halved

2 tbsp Thai fish sauce

fresh Thai basil sprigs and thinly sliced kaffir lime leaves, to garnish

Heat the oil in a preheated wok or large heavy-based frying pan. Add the curry paste and stir-fry briefly until all the aromas are released.

Add the chicken, lime leaves and lemon grass and stir-fry for 3–4 minutes, until the meat is beginning to colour. Add the coconut milk and aubergines and simmer gently for 8–10 minutes, or until tender.

Stir in the fish sauce and serve immediately, garnished with Thai basil sprigs and lime leaves.

PENANG CHICKEN CURRY

Heat the oil in a wok and stir-fry the onions for 1 minute. Add the curry paste and stir-fry for 1–2 minutes.

Pour in the coconut milk and stock. Add the lime leaves and lemon grass and simmer for 1 minute. Add the chicken and gradually bring to the boil. Simmer for 8–10 minutes, until the chicken is tender.

Stir in the fish sauce, soy sauce and sugar and simmer for 1–2 minutes. Stir in the peanuts, pineapple and cucumber and cook for 30 seconds. Serve immediately, sprinkled with extra peanuts and cucumber.

Serves 4

1 tbsp vegetable or groundnut oil

2 red onions, sliced

2 tbsp Penang curry paste

400 ml/14 fl oz coconut milk

150 ml/5 fl oz chicken stock

4 kaffir lime leaves, roughly torn

1 lemon grass stalk, finely chopped

6 skinless, boneless chicken thighs, chopped

1 tbsp Thai fish sauce

2 tbsp Thai soy sauce

1 tsp palm sugar or soft light brown sugar

50 g/1¾ oz unsalted peanuts, roasted and chopped, plus extra to garnish

175 g/6 oz fresh pineapple, roughly chopped

15-cm/6-inch piece cucumber, halved lengthways, peeled, deseeded and thickly sliced, plus extra to garnish

CAJUN CHICKEN

Preheat the barbecue. Using a sharp knife, make 2–3 diagonal slashes in the chicken drumsticks and thighs, then place them in a large dish. Cut the corn cobs into thick slices and add them to the dish. Mix all the ingredients for the spice mix together in a small bowl.

Brush the chicken and corn with the melted butter and sprinkle with the spice mix. Toss to coat well.

Cook the chicken over hot coals, turning occasionally, for 15 minutes, then add the corn slices and cook, turning occasionally, for a further 10–15 minutes, or until the chicken is cooked through and the corn is beginning to blacken slightly at the edges. Alternatively, cook in a ridged griddle pan or under a hot grill. Transfer to a large serving plate and serve immediately.

SRI LANKAN
CHICKEN CURRY

Cut the chicken into 5-cm/2-inch chunks and put them in a mixing bowl. Add the salt and vinegar, mix well and set aside for 30 minutes.

Preheat a small heavy-based pan over a medium heat and dry-roast the coriander seeds, cumin seeds, cinnamon, cloves, cardamom, fenugreek, chillies and curry leaves until they are dark but not black. Remove and cool, then grind in a spice grinder until finely ground. Set aside.

Heat the oil in a medium saucepan and cook the onion over a medium heat for 5 minutes, until translucent. Add the ginger and garlic purées and continue to cook for a further 2 minutes.

Add the turmeric, chilli powder, chicken and the ground spice mix. Stir and mix well, then add the lemon grass, tomatoes and warm water. Bring to the boil, reduce the heat to low, cover the pan and cook for 25 minutes.

Add the creamed coconut and stir until it has dissolved. Cook for 7–8 minutes, remove from the heat and serve with basmati rice.

Serves 4

700 g/1 lb 9 oz skinless, boneless chicken thighs or breasts

1 tsp salt, or to taste

2 tbsp white wine vinegar

2 tsp coriander seeds

1 tsp cumin seeds

2.5-cm/1-inch piece cinnamon stick, broken up

4 cloves

4 green cardamom pods

6 fenugreek seeds

4 dried red chillies, torn into pieces

10–12 curry leaves

4 tbsp sunflower or olive oil

1 large onion, finely chopped

2 tsp ginger purée

2 tsp garlic purée

1 tsp ground turmeric

½ tsp chilli powder

1 lemon grass stalk, finely sliced

200 g/7 oz canned chopped tomatoes

150 ml/5 fl oz warm water

55 g/2 oz creamed coconut, cut into small pieces

cooked basmati rice, to serve

JERK CHICKEN

Serves 4

4 lean chicken portions

1 bunch spring onions, trimmed

1–2 Scotch Bonnet chillies, deseeded

1 garlic clove

5-cm/2-inch piece fresh ginger, peeled and roughly chopped

½ tsp dried thyme

½ tsp paprika

¼ tsp ground allspice

pinch of ground cinnamon

pinch of ground cloves

4 tbsp white wine vinegar

3 tbsp light soy sauce

pepper

Rinse the chicken portions and pat them dry on absorbent kitchen paper. Place them in a shallow dish.

Place the spring onions, chillies, garlic, ginger, thyme, paprika, allspice, cinnamon, cloves, vinegar, soy sauce and pepper to taste in a food processor and process until smooth.

Pour the spice mixture over the chicken. Turn the chicken portions over so that they are well coated in the marinade. Transfer the chicken portions to the refrigerator and leave to marinate for up to 24 hours.

Preheat the barbecue. Remove the chicken from the marinade and cook over hot coals for about 30 minutes, turning the chicken over and basting occasionally with any remaining marinade, until the chicken is browned and cooked through. Alternatively, cook in a ridged griddle pan or under a hot grill.

Transfer the chicken portions to individual serving plates and serve at once.

ROAST CHICKEN WITH CUMIN BUTTER

Preheat the oven to 220°C/425°F/Gas Mark 7.
Mash together the butter, cumin seeds, preserved
lemon and garlic, and season to taste with salt
and pepper. Using your fingers, loosen the skin on
the chicken breasts and legs. Push most of the
flavoured butter under the skin, moulding it to the
shape of the bird. Smear any remaining butter
over the skin.

Place the chicken in a roasting tin and cook in
the preheated oven for 20 minutes. Reduce the
temperature to 180°C/350°F/Gas Mark 4 and
cook for a further 50–55 minutes, until the juices
run clear when you pierce the thickest part of the
chicken with a skewer. Transfer the chicken to a
warmed serving dish, cover loosely with foil and
leave to rest for 15 minutes.

Pour off most of the fat from the roasting tin. Place
the tin over a medium heat and cook the juices
for a few minutes, scraping any sediment from the
base of the tin, until reduced slightly. Carve the
chicken into slices, pour over the juices and serve
with roasted vegetables.

Serves 4

100 g/3½ oz butter, softened
½ tbsp cumin seeds, lightly crushed
½ preserved lemon, finely chopped
1 large garlic clove, crushed
1 whole chicken, about
1.5 kg/3 lb 5 oz
salt and pepper
roasted vegetables, to serve

FRIED CHILLI CHICKEN

Put the chicken in a non-metallic bowl and rub in the lemon juice and salt. Set aside for 30 minutes.

Meanwhile, purée the garlic, ginger, onion and red chillies in a food processor or blender. Add a little water, if necessary, to help blade movement in a blender.

Heat the oil in a wide shallow pan, preferably non-stick, over a medium–high heat. When the oil is hot, cook the chicken in two batches, until golden brown on all sides. Drain on kitchen paper.

Add the fresh spice paste to the pan with the turmeric and chilli powder and reduce the heat to medium. Cook for 5–6 minutes, stirring regularly.

Add the chicken and warm water. Bring to the boil, reduce the heat to low, cover and cook for 20 minutes. Increase the heat to medium, cover and cook for a further 8–10 minutes, stirring halfway through to ensure that the thickened sauce does not stick to the base of the pan.

Remove the lid and cook until the sauce is reduced to a paste-like consistency, stirring regularly to prevent the sauce from sticking. Add the green chillies, cook for 2–3 minutes, remove from the heat and serve with basmati rice.

LOUISIANA CHICKEN

Heat the oil in a large heavy-based saucepan or flameproof casserole. Add the chicken and cook over a medium heat, stirring, for 5–10 minutes, or until golden. Transfer the chicken to a plate with a slotted spoon.

Stir the flour into the oil and cook over a very low heat, stirring constantly, for 15 minutes, or until light golden. Do not let it burn. Add the onion, celery and green pepper and cook, stirring constantly, for 2 minutes. Add the garlic, thyme and chillies and cook, stirring, for 1 minute.

Stir in the tomatoes and their juices, then gradually stir in the stock. Return the chicken pieces to the saucepan, cover and simmer for 45 minutes, or until the chicken is cooked through and tender. Season to taste with salt and pepper, transfer to warmed serving plates and serve immediately, garnished with a sprinkling of chopped thyme.

Serves 4

5 tbsp sunflower oil

4 chicken portions

55 g/2 oz plain flour

1 onion, chopped

2 celery sticks, sliced

1 green pepper, deseeded and chopped

2 garlic cloves, finely chopped

2 tsp chopped fresh thyme, plus extra to garnish

2 fresh red chillies, deseeded and finely chopped

400 g/14 oz canned chopped tomatoes

300 ml/10 fl oz chicken stock

salt and pepper

SPICED ROAST POUSSINS

Serves 4

4 small poussins, weighing about 350–500 g/ 12 oz–1 lb 2 oz each

4 lemon grass stalks

4 fresh kaffir lime leaves

4 slices fresh ginger

about 6 tbsp coconut milk, for brushing

cooked basmati rice, to serve

fresh coriander sprigs and lime wedges, to garnish

Marinade

4 garlic cloves, peeled

2 fresh coriander sprigs

1 tbsp light soy sauce

salt and pepper

Preheat the oven to 190°C/375°F/Gas Mark 5. Carefully wash the poussins and pat dry on kitchen paper.

Place all the ingredients for the marinade in a blender and purée until smooth. Alternatively, grind to a paste with a pestle and mortar.

Rub the marinade mixture into the skin of the poussins, using the back of a spoon to spread it evenly.

Place a lemon grass stalk, a lime leaf and a piece of ginger in the cavity of each poussin.

Place the poussins in a roasting tin and brush lightly with the coconut milk. Roast in the preheated oven for about 30 minutes.

Remove from the oven, brush again with coconut milk, then return to the oven and cook for a further 15–25 minutes, or until golden and cooked through, depending on the size of the poussin. The poussins are cooked when the juices run clear when a skewer is inserted into the thickest part of the meat.

Serve the poussins with the pan juices poured over. Garnish with coriander sprigs and lime wedges and serve with rice.

MEXICAN TURKEY

Preheat the oven to 160°C/325°F/Gas Mark 3. Spread the flour on a plate and season to taste with salt and pepper. Coat the turkey fillets in the seasoned flour, shaking off any excess. Reserve the seasoned flour.

Heat the oil in a flameproof casserole. Add the turkey fillets and cook over a medium heat, turning occasionally, for 5–10 minutes, or until golden. Transfer to a plate with a slotted spoon.

Add the onion and red pepper to the casserole. Cook over a low heat, stirring occasionally, for 5 minutes, or until softened. Sprinkle in any remaining seasoned flour and cook, stirring constantly, for 1 minute. Gradually stir in the stock, then add the raisins, tomatoes, chilli powder, cinnamon, cumin and chocolate. Season to taste with salt and pepper. Bring to the boil, stirring constantly.

Return the turkey to the casserole, cover and cook in the preheated oven for 50 minutes. Serve immediately, garnished with coriander sprigs.

Serves 4

55 g/2 oz plain flour

4 turkey breast fillets

3 tbsp sunflower oil

1 onion, thinly sliced

1 red pepper, deseeded and sliced

300 ml/10 fl oz chicken stock

25 g/1 oz raisins

4 tomatoes, peeled, deseeded and chopped

1 tsp chilli powder

½ tsp ground cinnamon

pinch of ground cumin

25 g/1 oz plain chocolate, finely chopped or grated

salt and pepper

fresh coriander sprigs, to garnish

TURKEY & CASHEW NUT STIR-FRY

Mix together the cornflour and five-spice powder in a bowl and stir in the turkey. Add the soy sauce and sherry, stirring to coat. Set aside for 30 minutes.

Heat a wok or large frying pan over a high heat. Heat 2 tablespoons of the oil, then add the turkey mixture and stir-fry for 2–3 minutes, until golden and cooked through. Using a slotted spoon, transfer the turkey to a plate and keep warm.

Heat the remaining oil in the wok and stir-fry the garlic, ginger, spring onions and carrot for 1 minute. Return the turkey to the wok with the cashew nuts, hoisin sauce and salt. Reduce the heat to medium–high and stir-fry for a further minute. Sprinkle with shredded spring onion and serve immediately with rice.

DUCK BREASTS WITH CHILLI & LIME

To make the marinade, mix together the garlic, sugar, lime juice, soy sauce and chilli sauce.

Using a small sharp knife, cut deep slashes in the skin of the duck breasts to make a diamond pattern. Place the duck breasts in a wide non-metallic dish.

Spoon the marinade over the duck breasts, turning well to coat them evenly in the mixture. Cover the dish with clingfilm and leave to marinate in the refrigerator for at least 3 hours, or overnight if possible.

Drain the duck, reserving the marinade. Heat a large heavy-based pan until very hot and brush with the oil. Add the duck breasts, skin-side down, and cook for 4–5 minutes, until the skin is browned and crisp. Pour off the excess fat.

Turn the duck breasts and cook on the other side for 2–3 minutes to brown. Add the reserved marinade, the stock and jam and simmer for 2 minutes. Adjust the seasoning, adding salt and pepper to taste, and spoon the juices over the meat. Serve with rice and lime wedges.

Serves 4

4 boneless duck breasts

1 tsp vegetable oil

125 ml/4 fl oz chicken stock

2 tbsp plum jam

salt and pepper

cooked rice and lime wedges, to serve

Marinade

2 garlic cloves, crushed

4 tsp soft light brown sugar

3 tbsp lime juice

1 tbsp soy sauce

1 tsp chilli sauce

DUCK JAMBALAYA-STYLE STEW

Serves 4

4 duck breasts, about
150 g/5½ oz each

2 tbsp olive oil

225 g/8 oz gammon, cut into
small chunks

225 g/8 oz chorizo, outer
casing removed

1 onion, chopped

3 garlic cloves, chopped

3 celery sticks, chopped

1–2 fresh red chillies,
deseeded and chopped

1 green pepper, deseeded
and chopped

600 ml/1 pint chicken stock

1 tbsp chopped fresh oregano

400 g/14 oz canned chopped
tomatoes

1–2 tsp hot pepper sauce,
or to taste

chopped fresh flat-leaf parsley,
to garnish

green salad and cooked rice,
to serve

Remove and discard the skin and any fat from the duck breasts. Cut the flesh into bite-sized pieces.

Heat half the oil in a large deep frying pan and cook the duck, gammon and chorizo over a high heat, stirring frequently, for 5 minutes, or until browned on all sides and sealed. Using a slotted spoon, remove from the frying pan and set aside.

Add the onion, garlic, celery and chillies to the frying pan and cook over a medium heat, stirring frequently, for 5 minutes, or until softened. Add the green pepper, then stir in the stock, oregano, tomatoes and hot pepper sauce.

Bring to the boil, then reduce the heat and return the duck, gammon and chorizo to the frying pan. Cover and simmer, stirring occasionally, for 20 minutes, or until the duck and gammon are tender.

Serve immediately, garnished with parsley and accompanied by a green salad and rice.

ZESTY

Flavoursome fish & seafood

FISH WITH YUCATAN FLAVOURS

Drain the annatto, then crush them to a paste using a pestle and mortar. Work in the garlic, chilli powder, paprika, cumin, oregano, beer, lime and orange juices, oil, coriander, cinnamon and cloves.

Smear the paste onto the fish, cover and marinate in the refrigerator for at least 3 hours or overnight.

Wrap the fish steaks in banana leaves, if using, tying with string to make parcels. Bring enough water to the boil in a steamer, then add a batch of parcels to the top part of the steamer and steam for 15 minutes, or until the fish is cooked through.

Alternatively, cook the fish without wrapping in the banana leaves. To cook on the barbecue, place in a hinged basket, or on a rack, and cook over hot coals for 5–6 minutes on each side, or until cooked through. Alternatively, cook the fish under a preheated hot grill for 5–6 minutes on each side, or until cooked through.

Serve with orange wedges for squeezing over the fish.

Serves 8

4 tbsp annatto seeds, soaked in water overnight

3 garlic cloves, finely chopped

1 tbsp mild chilli powder

1 tbsp paprika

1 tsp ground cumin

½ tsp dried oregano

2 tbsp beer or tequila

juice of 1 lime and 1 orange or 3 tbsp pineapple juice

2 tbsp olive oil

2 tbsp chopped fresh coriander

¼ tsp ground cinnamon

¼ tsp ground cloves

1 kg/2 lb 4 oz swordfish steaks

banana leaves, for wrapping (optional)

orange wedges, to serve

SEA BREAM WITH CHILLI & GINGER

Rinse the fish fillets under cold running water, then pat dry with kitchen paper. Make several fairly deep diagonal cuts into the fish on both sides. Put the fish on a heatproof plate that is slightly smaller than your wok. The plate should have a rim.

In a separate bowl, mix together the garlic, chilli, fish sauce, lemon juice and stock. Pour this mixture over the fish. Scatter over the spring onions, lemon rind and ginger.

Fill a large wok with boiling water up to a depth of about 4 cm/1½ inches. Bring it back to the boil, then set a rack or trivet inside the wok. Put the plate of fish on top of the rack, then cover the wok with a lid. Reduce the heat a little and steam the fish for about 10 minutes, or until cooked through.

Lift out the fish and transfer to individual serving plates. Serve with the noodles and lemon wedges.

SWEET & SOUR SEA BASS

Preheat the oven to 200°C/400°F/Gas Mark 6. Cut out 2 x 38-cm/15-inch squares of greaseproof paper and 2 x 38-cm/15-inch squares of foil.

To make the sauce, heat the pineapple juice, sugar, vinegar, star anise and tomato juice and simmer for 1–2 minutes. Thicken with the cornflour and water mixture, whisking constantly, then pass through a fine sieve into a small bowl to cool.

In a separate large bowl mix together the pak choi, beansprouts, mushrooms and spring onions, then add the ginger and lemon grass. Toss all the ingredients together.

Put a square of greaseproof paper on top of a square of foil and fold into a triangle. Open up and place half the vegetable mix in the centre, pour half the sweet and sour sauce over the vegetables and place the sea bass on top. Sprinkle with a few sesame seeds. Close the triangle over the mixture and crumple the edges together to form an airtight triangular parcel. Repeat to make the second parcel.

Place the foil parcels on a baking tray and cook in the preheated oven for 10 minutes, until they puff with steam. To serve, place the parcels on individual plates and snip them open.

Serves 2

60 g/2¼ oz pak choi, shredded

40 g/1½ oz beansprouts

40 g/1½ oz shiitake mushrooms, sliced

40 g/1½ oz oyster mushrooms, torn

20 g/¾ oz spring onions, finely sliced

1 tsp finely grated fresh ginger

1 tbsp finely sliced lemon grass

2 x 90 g/3¼ oz sea bass fillets, skinned and boned

10 g/¼ oz sesame seeds, toasted

Sweet & sour sauce

90 ml/3 fl oz pineapple juice

1 tbsp sugar

1 tbsp red wine vinegar

2 star anise, crushed

90 ml/3 fl oz tomato juice

1 tbsp cornflour, blended with a little cold water

TUNA WITH CHILLI SALSA

Serves 4

4 tuna steaks,
about 175 g/6 oz each

grated rind and juice of 1 lime

2 tbsp olive oil

salt and pepper

fresh coriander sprigs,
to garnish

Chilli salsa

2 orange peppers

1 tbsp olive oil

juice of 1 lime

juice of 1 orange

2–3 fresh red chillies,
deseeded and chopped

pinch of cayenne pepper

salt and pepper

Rinse the tuna thoroughly under cold running water and pat dry with kitchen paper, then place in a large, shallow non-metallic dish. Sprinkle the lime rind and juice and the oil over the fish. Season to taste with salt and pepper, cover with clingfilm and leave to marinate in the refrigerator for up to 1 hour.

Preheat the barbecue. To make the salsa, brush the peppers with the oil and cook over hot coals, turning frequently, for 10 minutes, or until the skin is blackened and charred. Remove from the barbecue and leave to cool slightly, then peel off the skins and discard the stem and the seeds. Put the peppers into a food processor with the remaining salsa ingredients and process to a purée. Transfer to a bowl and season to taste with salt and pepper.

Cook the tuna over hot coals for 4–5 minutes on each side, until golden. Alternatively, cook in a ridged griddle pan or under a hot grill. Transfer to serving plates, garnish with coriander sprigs and serve with the salsa.

133

SICILIAN TUNA

Whisk all the marinade ingredients together in a small bowl. Put the tuna steaks in a large, shallow dish and spoon over 4 tablespoons of the marinade, turning until well coated. Cover and leave to marinate in the refrigerator for 30 minutes. Reserve the remaining marinade.

Heat a ridged griddle pan over a high heat. Put the fennel and onions in a separate bowl, add the oil and toss well to coat. Add to the griddle pan and cook for 5 minutes on each side, until just beginning to colour. Transfer to 4 warmed serving plates, drizzle with the reserved marinade and keep warm.

Add the tuna steaks to the griddle pan and cook, turning once, for 4–5 minutes, until firm to the touch but still moist inside. Transfer the tuna to the serving plates and serve immediately.

Serves 4

4 tuna steaks, about 140 g/5 oz each

2 fennel bulbs, thickly sliced lengthways

2 red onions, sliced

2 tbsp extra virgin olive oil

Marinade

125 ml/4 fl oz extra virgin olive oil

4 garlic cloves, finely chopped

4 fresh red chillies, deseeded and finely chopped

juice and finely grated rind of 2 lemons

4 tbsp finely chopped fresh flat-leaf parsley

salt and pepper

SPICY GRILLED SALMON

To make the marinade, finely chop the garlic and place in a non-metallic bowl with the oil, allspice, cinnamon, lime juice, chipotle marinade, cumin and sugar. Add salt and pepper to taste and stir to combine.

Coat the salmon with the marinade, then transfer to a large non-metallic dish. Cover with clingfilm and leave to marinate in the refrigerator for 1 hour.

Preheat the grill to medium. Transfer the salmon to the grill rack and cook under the preheated grill for 3–4 minutes on each side, or until cooked through. Alternatively, cook the salmon over hot coals on a barbecue until cooked through.

Place the salmon on individual serving plates, garnish with lime slices and serve with a mixed salad.

SALMON POTATO PATTIES WITH JALAPEÑOS

Cook the potatoes in a large saucepan of lightly salted boiling water for 15 minutes, or until tender.

Meanwhile, lightly poach the salmon fillet in a saucepan of gently simmering water for 5–6 minutes (if in one piece), or until just cooked but still moist. Alternatively, cut into 4 equal-sized pieces and cook in a microwave oven on medium for 3 minutes, then turn the pieces around so that the cooked parts are in the centre, and cook for a further 1–2 minutes – check after 1 minute; the fish should be barely cooked. Using a fork, flake the flesh into a bowl.

Drain the potatoes, return to the saucepan and, while still warm, roughly mash with a fork, adding the mayonnaise, egg and milk, if needed – the mixture must remain firm, so only add the milk if necessary. Stir in the chillies, coriander leaves and salt and pepper to taste, then lightly mix in the salmon flakes.

With floured hands, form the mixture into 8 small patties. Heat the oil in a large non-stick frying pan over a medium–high heat, add the patties and cook for 5 minutes on each side, or until golden brown. Carefully remove with a fish slice and serve immediately.

Serves 4

400 g/14 oz potatoes, cut into medium-sized chunks

400 g/14 oz skinless salmon fillet

2 tbsp mayonnaise

1 egg, beaten

dash of milk, if needed

2 fresh red jalapeño chillies, deseeded and finely chopped

1 small bunch fresh coriander leaves

plain flour, for dusting

1 tbsp olive oil

salt and pepper

GOAN FISH CURRY

Serves 4

4 skinless salmon fillets, about 200 g/7 oz each

1 tsp salt, or to taste

1 tbsp lemon juice

3 tbsp sunflower or olive oil

1 large onion, finely chopped

2 tsp garlic purée

2 tsp ginger purée

½ tsp ground turmeric

1 tsp ground coriander

½ tsp ground cumin

½–1 tsp chilli powder

250 ml/9 fl oz coconut milk

2–3 fresh green chillies, sliced lengthways (deseeded if you like)

2 tbsp cider vinegar or white wine vinegar

2 tbsp chopped fresh coriander leaves

cooked basmati rice, to serve

Cut each salmon fillet in half and lay on a plate in a single layer. Sprinkle with half the salt and all of the lemon juice and rub in gently. Cover and leave to marinate in the refrigerator for 15–20 minutes.

Heat the oil in a frying pan over a medium heat, add the onion and cook, stirring frequently to ensure even colouring, for 8–9 minutes, until a pale golden colour.

Add the garlic and ginger purées and cook, stirring, for 1 minute, then add the turmeric, ground coriander, cumin and chilli powder and cook, stirring, for 1 minute. Add the coconut milk, chillies and vinegar, then the remaining salt, stir well and simmer, uncovered, for 6–8 minutes.

Add the fish and cook gently for 5–6 minutes. Stir in the fresh coriander and remove from the heat. Serve immediately with basmati rice.

PENANG FISH CURRY

Put the peanuts, shallots, chillies, ginger, garlic and shrimp paste in a food processor or blender and blend until the mixture is mushy. Remove and set aside.

Heat the oil in a large shallow pan, preferably non-stick, and add the peanut mixture, turmeric and chilli powder. Cook over a medium heat, stirring regularly, until the mixture begins to brown, then continue to cook until the mixture is fragrant, adding a little water from time to time to prevent the mixture from sticking to the base of the pan. This process will take 10–12 minutes.

Pour in the warm water and add the salt, tamarind juice and sugar. Stir and mix well and carefully add the fish. Stir gently to ensure that the fish is covered with the sauce. Cover the pan, reduce the heat to low and cook for 8–10 minutes. Remove from the heat and serve garnished with coriander sprigs and accompanied by basmati rice.

Serves 4

25 g/1 oz dry roasted peanuts

8–10 shallots or 2 onions, roughly chopped

2–3 fresh red chillies, roughly chopped

2.5-cm/1-inch piece fresh ginger, roughly chopped

4 large garlic cloves, roughly chopped

1 tsp shrimp paste

4 tbsp groundnut oil

1 tsp ground turmeric

½ tsp chilli powder

425 ml/15 fl oz warm water

½ tsp salt, or to taste

2 tbsp tamarind juice

½ tsp sugar

700 g/1 lb 9 oz trout fillets, cut into 1-cm/½-inch slices

fresh coriander sprigs, to garnish

cooked basmati rice, to serve

THAI GREEN FISH CURRY

Heat the oil in a large frying pan or preheated wok over a medium heat until almost smoking. Add the garlic and cook until golden. Add the curry paste and stir-fry for a few seconds before adding the aubergine. Stir-fry for about 4–5 minutes, until soft.

Add the coconut milk, bring to the boil and stir until it thickens and curdles slightly. Add the fish sauce and sugar to the frying pan and stir well.

Add the fish pieces and stock. Simmer for 3–4 minutes, stirring occasionally, until the fish is just tender. Add the lime leaves and basil, then cook for a further minute. Transfer to a warmed serving dish and garnish with dill sprigs. Serve immediately.

BALTI FISH CURRY

To make the marinade, mix the garlic and ginger paste, green chilli, ground coriander, cumin, turmeric and chilli powder together with salt to taste in a large bowl. Gradually stir in the water to form a thin paste. Add the fish chunks and smear with the marinade. Tuck the bay leaves underneath and leave to marinate in the refrigerator for at least 30 minutes, or up to 4 hours.

When you are ready to cook the fish, remove from the refrigerator 15 minutes in advance. Melt the ghee in a wok or large frying pan over a medium–high heat. Add the onions, sprinkle with the salt and cook, stirring frequently, for 8 minutes, or until they are very soft and golden.

Gently add the fish with its marinade and the bay leaves to the pan and stir in the water. Bring to the boil, then immediately reduce the heat and cook the fish for 4–5 minutes, spooning the sauce over the fish and carefully moving the chunks around, until they are cooked through and the flesh flakes easily. Garnish with fresh coriander and serve with Indian bread.

Serves 4–6

900 g/2 lb thick fish fillets, such as monkfish, grey mullet, cod or haddock, rinsed and cut into large chunks

2 bay leaves, torn

140 g/5 oz ghee or 150 ml/5 fl oz vegetable or groundnut oil

2 large onions, chopped

½ tbsp salt

150 ml/5 fl oz water

chopped fresh coriander, to garnish

Indian bread, to serve

Marinade

½ tbsp garlic and ginger paste

1 fresh green chilli, deseeded and chopped

1 tsp ground coriander

1 tsp ground cumin

½ tsp ground turmeric

¼–½ tsp chilli powder

1 tbsp water

salt

MIXED SEAFOOD CURRY

Serves 4

1 tbsp vegetable or groundnut oil

3 shallots, finely chopped

2.5-cm/1-inch piece fresh galangal, peeled and thinly sliced

2 garlic cloves, finely chopped

400 ml/14 fl oz coconut milk

2 lemon grass stalks, snapped in half

4 tbsp Thai fish sauce

2 tbsp chilli sauce

225 g/8 oz raw tiger prawns, peeled and deveined

225 g/8 oz baby squid, cleaned and thickly sliced

225 g/8 oz salmon fillet, skinned and cut into chunks

175 g/6 oz tuna steak, cut into chunks

225 g/8 oz fresh mussels, scrubbed and debearded

lime wedges, to garnish

cooked rice, to serve

Heat the oil in a large wok with a tight-fitting lid and stir-fry the shallots, galangal and garlic for 1–2 minutes, until they start to soften. Add the coconut milk, lemon grass, fish sauce and chilli sauce. Bring to the boil, lower the heat and simmer for 1–2 minutes.

Add the prawns, squid, salmon and tuna and simmer for 3–4 minutes, until the prawns have turned pink and the fish is cooked.

Discard any mussels with broken shells and any that refuse to close when tapped with a knife. Add the remaining mussels to the wok and cover with a lid. Simmer for 1–2 minutes, until they have opened. Discard any mussels that remain closed. Garnish with lime wedges and serve immediately with rice.

149

GOAN-STYLE SEAFOOD CURRY

Heat the oil in a kadhai, wok or large frying pan over a high heat. Add the mustard seeds and stir them around for about 1 minute, or until they jump. Stir in the curry leaves.

Add the shallots and garlic and stir for about 5 minutes, or until the shallots are golden. Stir in the turmeric, coriander and chilli powder and continue stirring for about 30 seconds.

Add the dissolved creamed coconut. Bring to the boil, then reduce the heat to medium and stir for about 2 minutes.

Reduce the heat to low, add the fish and simmer for 1 minute, spooning the sauce over the fish and very gently stirring it around. Add the prawns and continue to simmer for a further 4–5 minutes, until the fish flesh flakes easily and the prawns turn pink and curl.

Add half the lime juice, then taste and add more lime juice and salt to taste. Sprinkle with the lime rind and serve with lime wedges.

Serves 4–6

3 tbsp vegetable or groundnut oil

1 tbsp black mustard seeds

12 fresh curry leaves or 1 tbsp dried

6 shallots, finely chopped

1 garlic clove, crushed

1 tsp ground turmeric

½ tsp ground coriander

¼–½ tsp chilli powder

140 g/5 oz creamed coconut, grated and dissolved in 300 ml/10 fl oz boiling water

500 g/1 lb 2 oz skinless, boneless white fish, such as monkfish or cod, cut into large chunks

450 g/1 lb large raw prawns, peeled and deveined

finely grated rind and juice of 1 lime

salt

lime wedges, to serve

CHILLI PRAWNS WITH NOODLES

Toss the prawns with the chilli sauce in a bowl. Cover and set aside.

Heat half the oil in a preheated wok, add the spring onions and mangetout and stir-fry over a medium–high heat for 2–3 minutes. Add the curry paste and stir well. Pour in the coconut milk and bring gently to the boil, stirring occasionally. Add the bamboo shoots and beansprouts and cook, stirring, for 1 minute. Stir in the prawns and chilli sauce, reduce the heat and simmer for 1–2 minutes, until just heated through.

Meanwhile, cook the noodles in a saucepan of lightly salted boiling water for 4–5 minutes, or according to the packet instructions, until just tender. Drain and return to the saucepan.

Heat the remaining oil in a small non-stick frying pan, add the garlic and stir-fry over a high heat for 30 seconds. Add to the drained noodles with half the coriander and toss together until well mixed.

Transfer the noodles to 4 serving bowls, top with the prawn mixture and serve immediately, garnished with the remaining coriander.

THAI SWORDFISH KEBABS

Put the swordfish, red peppers and onion in a non-metallic dish. Finely grate the rind (without pith) from one of the limes and add to the dish, then squeeze the juice from both limes and add to the dish along with all the remaining ingredients. Stir well, cover and leave to marinate in a cool place for 30 minutes–1 hour, if possible.

Preheat the grill to high or preheat the barbecue. Thread the swordfish, red peppers and onion alternately onto 4 metal or pre-soaked wooden skewers. Cook the kebabs under the grill or over the barbecue for 8 minutes, turning halfway through and spooning over any remaining marinade as you do so. Serve immediately, garnished with lime wedges.

Serves 4

700 g/1 lb 9 oz swordfish steaks, cut into bite-sized chunks

2 red peppers, deseeded and cut into bite-sized squares

1 red onion, cut into bite-sized chunks

2 limes

2 garlic cloves, finely chopped

2 tsp chopped fresh ginger

2 fresh red chillies, deseeded and finely chopped

1 tsp dried lemon grass

2 tbsp sesame oil

1 handful of fresh coriander leaves, chopped

lime wedges, to garnish

MOROCCAN FISH TAGINE

Serves 4

2 tbsp olive oil

1 large onion, finely chopped

pinch of saffron threads

½ tsp ground cinnamon

1 tsp ground coriander

½ tsp ground cumin

½ tsp ground turmeric

200 g/7 oz canned chopped tomatoes

300 ml/10 fl oz fish stock

4 small red mullet, cleaned, boned and heads and tails removed

55 g/2 oz stoned green olives

1 tbsp chopped preserved lemon

3 tbsp chopped fresh coriander

salt and pepper

cooked couscous, to serve

Heat the oil in a flameproof casserole. Add the onion and cook gently over a very low heat, stirring occasionally, for 10 minutes, or until softened but not coloured. Add the saffron, cinnamon, ground coriander, cumin and turmeric and cook for a further 30 seconds, stirring constantly.

Add the tomatoes and stock and stir well. Bring to the boil, reduce the heat, cover and simmer for 15 minutes. Uncover and simmer for 20–35 minutes, or until thickened.

Cut each red mullet in half, then add the fish pieces to the casserole, pushing them down into the liquid. Simmer the stew for a further 5–6 minutes, or until the fish is just cooked.

Carefully stir in the olives, preserved lemon and chopped coriander. Season to taste with salt and pepper and serve immediately with couscous.

157

SEAFOOD CHILLI

Place the prawns, scallops, monkfish chunks and lime slices in a large non-metallic dish with ¼ teaspoon of the chilli powder, ¼ teaspoon of the cumin, 1 tablespoon of the chopped coriander, half the garlic, the fresh chilli and 1 tablespoon of the oil. Cover with clingfilm and leave to marinate for up to 1 hour.

Meanwhile, heat 1 tablespoon of the remaining oil in a flameproof casserole or large heavy-based saucepan. Add the onion, the remaining garlic and the red and yellow peppers and cook over a low heat, stirring occasionally, for 5 minutes, or until softened. Add the remaining chilli powder, the remaining cumin, the cloves, cinnamon and cayenne pepper with the remaining oil, if necessary, and season to taste with salt. Cook, stirring, for 5 minutes, then gradually stir in the stock and the tomatoes and their juices. Partially cover and simmer for 25 minutes.

Add the beans to the tomato mixture and spoon the monkfish, prawns and scallops on top. Cover and cook for 10 minutes, or until the fish and shellfish are cooked through. Sprinkle with the remaining coriander and serve.

Serves 4

115 g/4 oz raw prawns, peeled

250 g/9 oz prepared scallops, thawed if frozen

115 g/4 oz monkfish fillet, cut into chunks

1 lime, peeled and thinly sliced

1 tbsp chilli powder

1 tsp ground cumin

3 tbsp chopped fresh coriander

2 garlic cloves, finely chopped

1 fresh green chilli, deseeded and chopped

3 tbsp sunflower oil

1 onion, roughly chopped

1 red pepper, deseeded and roughly chopped

1 yellow pepper, deseeded and roughly chopped

¼ tsp ground cloves

pinch of ground cinnamon

pinch of cayenne pepper

350 ml/12 fl oz fish stock

400 g/14 oz canned chopped tomatoes

400 g/14 oz canned red kidney beans, drained and rinsed

salt

PRAWN & CHICKEN PAELLA

Discard any mussels with broken shells and any that refuse to close when tapped. Soak in lightly salted water for 10 minutes. Put the saffron and water in a cup and leave to infuse for a few minutes. Meanwhile, put the rice in a sieve and rinse in cold water until the water runs clear.

Heat 3 tablespoons of the oil in a paella pan or ovenproof casserole. Cook the chicken over medium-high heat, turning frequently, for 5 minutes, or until golden. Transfer to a bowl. Add the chorizo to the pan and cook, stirring, for 1 minute, or until beginning to crisp. Add to the chicken.

Heat the remaining oil in the pan and cook the onions, stirring frequently, for 2 minutes, then add the garlic and paprika and cook for a further 3 minutes, or until the onions are softened but not browned.

Add the drained rice, beans and peas and stir until coated in oil. Return the chicken and chorizo with any juices to the pan. Stir in the stock, saffron and its soaking liquid, and salt and pepper to taste and bring to the boil, stirring. Reduce the heat to low and simmer, uncovered and without stirring, for 15 minutes, or until the rice is almost tender and most of the liquid has been absorbed.

Arrange the mussels, prawns and red peppers on top, then cover and simmer, without stirring, for a further 5 minutes, or until the prawns turn pink and the mussels open. Discard any mussels that remain closed. Taste and adjust the seasoning if necessary. Sprinkle with the parsley and serve immediately.

LINGUINE WITH OLIVES, ANCHOVIES & CAPERS

Heat the oil in a heavy-based saucepan. Add the garlic and cook over a low heat, stirring frequently, for 2 minutes. Add the anchovies and mash them to a pulp with a fork. Add the olives, capers and tomatoes and season to taste with cayenne pepper. Cover and simmer for 25 minutes.

Meanwhile, bring a saucepan of lightly salted water to the boil. Add the pasta, bring back to the boil and cook for 8–10 minutes, until tender but still firm to the bite. Drain and transfer to a warmed serving dish.

Spoon the anchovy sauce into the dish and toss the pasta, using 2 large forks. Garnish with the parsley and serve immediately.

Serves 4

3 tbsp olive oil

2 garlic cloves, finely chopped

10 anchovy fillets, drained and chopped

140 g/5 oz black olives, stoned and chopped

1 tbsp capers, rinsed

450 g/1 lb plum tomatoes, peeled, deseeded and chopped

pinch of cayenne pepper

400 g/14 oz dried linguine

salt

2 tbsp chopped fresh flat-leaf parsley, to garnish

FRESH SARDINES WITH CHERMOULA

Serves 4

12 sardines, heads removed, cleaned and rinsed

olive oil, for brushing

sea salt, for sprinkling

lemon wedges, to serve

Chermoula

40 g/1½ oz fresh coriander leaves, plus extra to garnish

25 g/1 oz fresh flat-leaf parsley leaves

1½ tbsp ground cumin

1 tsp smoked paprika

½ tsp cayenne pepper, or to taste

3 tbsp freshly squeezed lemon juice

1 tsp salt

about 3 tbsp olive oil

To make the chermoula, put the herbs, spices, lemon juice and salt in a food processor and process until finely chopped and blended. Add 3 tablespoons of oil and process again to a thick sauce, adding extra oil, if necessary.

Spread 1 teaspoon of the chermoula on the inside of each sardine. Cover and leave to marinate at room temperature for 15 minutes or in the refrigerator for 2 4 hours.

Heat a ridged griddle pan over a very high heat until a splash of water 'dances' on the surface or preheat the grill to high. Brush the sardines with oil and lightly sprinkle with sea salt.

Brush the griddle pan or grill rack with oil, add the sardines and cook for 3 minutes. Use a fish slice to turn the sardines over, then sprinkle with more salt and cook for a further 2 minutes, or until slightly charred and cooked through. Be prepared for some sardine skin to stick to the griddle pan or grill rack. Garnish with coriander leaves and serve immediately with lemon wedges for squeezing over.

SEAFOOD PASTA PARCELS

Heat half the oil in a large saucepan. Add half the chillies and half the garlic, then add the pieces of crab shell. Cook over a medium heat, stirring, for 2–3 minutes. Add the tomatoes and wine. Reduce the heat and simmer for about 1 hour. Strain the sauce through a sieve. Season to taste with salt and pepper and set aside.

Bring a large saucepan of lightly salted water to the boil. Add the pasta, bring back to the boil and cook for 8–10 minutes, until the pasta is tender but still firm to the bite. Drain.

Heat the remaining oil with the butter in a large saucepan. Add the remaining chilli and garlic and cook over a low heat, stirring occasionally, for 5 minutes, until soft. Add the squid, prawns and mussels, cover and cook over a high heat for 4–5 minutes, until the mussels have opened. Add the crabmeat and heat through for 2–3 minutes. Remove from the heat and discard any mussels that remain closed. Stir in the pasta with the tomato sauce, parsley and basil, tossing well to coat.

Preheat the oven to 180°C/350°F/Gas Mark 4. Cut out 4 large squares of baking paper. Divide the pasta and seafood between them, fold in half and turn in the edges to seal. Transfer to a baking tray and bake in the preheated oven for 10 minutes, until the parcels have puffed up. Serve immediately, garnished with the basil sprigs.

Serves 4

2 tbsp extra virgin olive oil

2 fresh red chillies, deseeded and finely chopped

4 garlic cloves, finely chopped

1.5 kg/3 lb 5 oz freshly cooked crabmeat, shells reserved and broken into large pieces

800 g/1 lb 12 oz canned chopped tomatoes

225 ml/8 fl oz dry white wine

350 g/12 oz dried spaghetti

2 tbsp butter

115 g/4 oz prepared squid, sliced

175 g/6 oz raw Mediterranean prawns

450 g/1 lb live mussels, scrubbed and debearded (discard any with broken shells and any that refuse to close when tapped)

3 tbsp roughly chopped fresh flat-leaf parsley

1 tbsp shredded fresh basil leaves, plus extra sprigs to garnish

salt and pepper

PRAWNS WITH CITRUS SALSA

Preheat the barbecue. To make the salsa, peel the orange and cut into segments. Reserve any juice. Put the orange segments, apple quarters, chillies, garlic, coriander sprigs and mint sprigs into a food processor and process until smooth. With the motor running, add the lime juice through the feeder tube. Transfer the salsa to a serving bowl and season to taste with salt and pepper. Cover with clingfilm and leave to chill in the refrigerator until required.

Using a sharp knife, remove and discard the heads from the prawns, then peel off the shells. Cut along the back of the prawns and remove the dark intestinal vein. Rinse the prawns under cold running water and pat dry with kitchen paper. Mix the chopped coriander, cayenne and oil together in a dish. Add the prawns and toss well to coat.

Cook the prawns over hot coals for 3 minutes on each side, or until they have changed colour. Alternatively, cook in a ridged griddle pan or under a hot grill. Transfer to a large serving plate, garnish with fresh coriander leaves and serve immediately with lemon wedges and the salsa.

SPAGHETTI WITH CRAB & CHILLI

Using a sharp knife, scoop the meat from the crab shell into a bowl. Mix the white and brown meat together lightly and reserve.

Bring a large pan of lightly salted water to the boil over a medium heat. Add the pasta and cook for 8–10 minutes, or until tender but still firm to the bite. Drain thoroughly and return to the pan.

Meanwhile, heat 2 tablespoons of the oil in a frying pan over a low heat. Add the chilli and garlic and cook for 30 seconds, then add the crabmeat, parsley, lemon juice and lemon rind. Cook for 1 minute, until the crab is just heated through.

Add the crab mixture to the pasta with the remaining oil and season to taste with salt and pepper. Toss together thoroughly, transfer to a large warmed serving dish and garnish with lemon wedges. Serve immediately.

Serves 4

1 dressed crab, about 450 g/ 1 lb including the shell

350 g/12 oz dried spaghetti

6 tbsp extra virgin olive oil

1 fresh red chilli, deseeded and finely chopped

2 garlic cloves, finely chopped

3 tbsp chopped fresh parsley

2 tbsp lemon juice

1 tsp finely grated lemon rind

salt and pepper

lemon wedges, to garnish

SCALLOPS MEXICANA

Serves 4

2 tbsp butter

2 tbsp extra virgin olive oil

650 g/1 lb 7 oz scallops, shelled

4–5 spring onions, thinly sliced

3–4 garlic cloves, finely chopped

½ fresh green chilli, deseeded and finely chopped

2 tbsp finely chopped fresh coriander

juice of ½ lime

salt and pepper

lime wedges, to serve

Heat half the butter and half the oil in a large heavy-based frying pan until the butter foams.

Add the scallops and cook quickly until just turning opaque; do not overcook. Remove from the pan with a slotted spoon and keep warm.

Add the remaining butter and oil to the pan, then toss in the spring onions and garlic and cook over a medium heat until the spring onions are wilted. Return the scallops to the pan.

Remove the pan from the heat and add the chilli and coriander. Squeeze in the lime juice. Season to taste with salt and pepper and stir to mix well.

Serve immediately with lime wedges for squeezing over the scallops.

FRIED SQUID RINGS

Heat enough oil for deep-frying in a deep-fat fryer or heavy-based frying pan to 180–190°C/ 350–375°F, or until a cube of bread browns in 30 seconds.

Meanwhile, put the flour, paprika and salt and white pepper to taste in a polythene bag and shake together. Add the squid rings, and tentacles, if using, and shake until well coated. Use tongs to remove the squid pieces from the bag, shaking off any excess flour.

Add the squid pieces to the hot oil, in batches to avoid overcrowding, and cook, turning occasionally, for 3 minutes, or until golden brown. Remove with a slotted spoon and drain on a plate lined with crumpled kitchen paper. Keep hot in a low oven while you cook the remaining squid pieces. Make sure that the oil returns to the correct temperature between batches and remove any stray pieces of coating from the oil.

Garnish with coriander sprigs and serve hot.

Serves 4–6

olive oil, for deep-frying

about 100 g/3½ oz plain flour

pinch of hot paprika or chilli powder

600 g/1 lb 5 oz squid rings, and tentacles if available, rinsed and patted dry

salt and white pepper

fresh coriander sprigs, to garnish

FIERY

Delicious vegetable dishes

CHILLI BEAN STEW

Heat the oil in a large heavy-based saucepan with a tight-fitting lid and cook the onion, garlic and chillies, stirring frequently, for 5 minutes, or until softened. Add the kidney beans, cannellini beans and chickpeas. Blend the tomato purée with a little of the stock in a jug and pour over the bean mixture, then add the remaining stock. Bring to the boil, then reduce the heat and simmer for 10–15 minutes.

Add the red pepper, tomatoes, broad beans, and pepper to taste and simmer for a further 15–20 minutes, or until all the vegetables are tender. Stir in the chopped coriander.

Serve the stew topped with spoonfuls of soured cream and garnished with chopped coriander and a pinch of paprika.

Serves 4–6

2 tbsp olive oil

1 onion, chopped

2–4 garlic cloves, chopped

2 fresh red chillies, deseeded and sliced

225 g/8 oz canned kidney beans, drained and rinsed

225 g/8 oz canned cannellini beans, drained and rinsed

225 g/8 oz canned chickpeas, drained and rinsed

1 tbsp tomato purée

700–850 ml/1¼–1½ pints vegetable stock

1 red pepper, deseeded and chopped

4 tomatoes, roughly chopped

175 g/6 oz frozen or shelled fresh broad beans, thawed if frozen

1 tbsp chopped fresh coriander, plus extra to garnish

pepper

soured cream, to serve

paprika, to garnish

AUBERGINE TAGINE

Serves 2

1 aubergine, cut into 1-cm/½-inch cubes

3 tbsp olive oil

1 large onion, thinly sliced

1 carrot, diced

2 garlic cloves, chopped

115 g/4 oz brown-cap mushrooms, sliced

2 tsp ground coriander

2 tsp cumin seeds

1 tsp chilli powder

1 tsp ground turmeric

600 g/1 lb 5 oz canned chopped tomatoes

1.5 litres/2¾ pints vegetable stock

1 tbsp tomato purée

75 g/2¾ oz ready-to-eat dried apricots, roughly chopped

400 g/14 oz canned chickpeas, drained and rinsed

200 g/7 oz instant polenta

2 tbsp chopped fresh coriander, to garnish

Preheat the grill to medium. Toss the aubergine in 1 tablespoon of the oil and arrange in the grill pan. Cook under the preheated grill for 20 minutes, turning occasionally, until softened and beginning to blacken around the edges – brush with more oil if the aubergine becomes too dry.

Heat the remaining oil in a large heavy-based saucepan over a medium heat. Add the onion and fry, stirring occasionally, for 8 minutes, or until soft and golden. Add the carrot, garlic and mushrooms and cook for 5 minutes. Add the spices and cook, stirring constantly, for a further minute.

Add the tomatoes and 300 ml/10 fl oz of the stock, stir well, then add the tomato purée. Bring to the boil, then reduce the heat and simmer for 10 minutes, or until the sauce begins to thicken and reduce.

Add the aubergine, apricots and chickpeas, partially cover and cook for a further 10 minutes, stirring occasionally.

Meanwhile, pour the remaining stock into a non-stick saucepan and bring to the boil. Pour in the polenta in a steady stream, stirring constantly with a wooden spoon. Reduce the heat to low and cook for 1–2 minutes, or until the polenta thickens to a mashed-potato consistency. Serve the tagine with the polenta, sprinkled with the fresh coriander.

SPICY FRAGRANT BLACK BEAN CHILLI

Soak the beans overnight, then drain. Place in a saucepan, cover with water and bring to the boil. Boil for 10 minutes, then reduce the heat and simmer for 1½ hours, or until tender. Drain well, reserving 250 ml/8 fl oz of the cooking liquid.

Heat the oil in a frying pan. Add the onion and garlic and cook for 2 minutes, stirring, until softened.

Stir in the cumin and chilli powder and continue to cook for 20–30 seconds. Add the red pepper, carrot and tomatoes. Cook over a medium heat for 5 minutes.

Add half the coriander and the beans and their reserved liquid. Season to taste with salt and pepper. Simmer for 30–45 minutes, or until very flavourful and thickened.

Stir in the remaining coriander, season to taste with salt and pepper and serve at once.

Serves 4

400 g/14 oz dried black beans

2 tbsp olive oil

1 onion, chopped

5 garlic cloves, roughly chopped

½–1 tsp ground cumin

½–1 tsp mild chilli powder

1 red pepper, deseeded and diced

1 carrot, diced

400 g/14 oz fresh tomatoes, diced

1 bunch fresh coriander, roughly chopped

salt and pepper

SPICY CHICKPEA CASSEROLE

Dry-fry the seeds in a heavy-based frying pan for a few seconds, until aromatic. Add the oregano and cook for a further few seconds. Remove from the heat, transfer to a mortar and crush with a pestle.

Heat the oil in a large flameproof casserole. Cook the onions, red pepper and aubergine for 10 minutes, until soft. Add the ground seed mixture, garlic and chilli and cook for a further 2 minutes.

Add the tomatoes, chickpeas, green beans and stock. Bring to the boil, then cover and simmer gently for 1 hour. Stir in the coriander and serve immediately.

Serves 6

VEGETABLE GOULASH

Put the sun-dried tomatoes in a small heatproof bowl, cover with almost-boiling water and leave to soak for 15–20 minutes. Drain, reserving the soaking liquid.

Heat the oil in a large heavy-based saucepan with a tight-fitting lid and cook the chillies, garlic and vegetables, stirring frequently, for 5–8 minutes, until softened. Blend the tomato purée with a little of the stock in a jug and pour over the vegetable mixture, then add the remaining stock, lentils, the sun-dried tomatoes and their soaking liquid, the paprika and thyme.

Bring to the boil, then reduce the heat, cover and simmer for 15 minutes. Add the tomatoes and simmer for a further 15 minutes, or until the vegetables and lentils are tender. Serve topped with spoonfuls of soured cream, accompanied by crusty bread.

Serves 4

15 g/½ oz sun-dried tomatoes, chopped

2 tbsp olive oil

½–1 tsp crushed dried chillies

2–3 garlic cloves, chopped

1 large onion, cut into small wedges

1 small celeriac, cut into small chunks

225 g/8 oz carrots, sliced

225 g/8 oz new potatoes, scrubbed and cut into chunks

1 small acorn squash, deseeded, peeled and cut into small chunks, about 225 g/8 oz prepared weight

2 tbsp tomato purée

300 ml/10 fl oz vegetable stock

450 g/1 lb canned Puy or green lentils, drained and rinsed

1–2 tsp hot paprika

a few fresh thyme sprigs

450 g/1 lb ripe tomatoes

soured cream and crusty bread, to serve

SPRING VEGETABLE RICE

Serves 4

2 tbsp groundnut or vegetable oil

2 shallots, chopped

2 garlic cloves, crushed

225 g/8 oz basmati rice

600 ml/1 pint chicken stock

1 tbsp Thai red curry paste

1 tsp Thai fish sauce

3 tbsp soy sauce

175 g/6 oz baby corn, halved lengthways

115 g/4 oz baby carrots, halved lengthways

55 g/2 oz sugar snap peas

55 g/2 oz fresh beansprouts

4 tbsp sesame seeds

handful of fresh coriander, chopped

2 tbsp sesame oil

salt

Heat the oil in a preheated wok, add the shallots and garlic and stir-fry over a medium–high heat for 1–2 minutes. Add the rice and stir-fry for 2–3 minutes. Add the stock, curry paste, fish sauce and soy sauce and bring to the boil, stirring occasionally. Reduce the heat and simmer for 10–12 minutes, until the rice is tender, adding more stock or boiling water, if necessary,

Meanwhile, cook the baby corn and carrots in a saucepan of lightly salted boiling water for 2–3 minutes, until just tender. Add the sugar snap peas and cook for 1 minute. Add the beansprouts, stir well, then drain.

Heat a dry frying pan until hot, add the sesame seeds and cook over a medium–high heat, shaking the frying pan frequently, for 30–45 seconds, until lightly browned.

Add the drained vegetables, coriander and sesame oil to the rice and serve immediately, scattered with the toasted sesame seeds.

189

MUSHROOM STROGANOFF

Heat the butter in a large heavy-based frying pan. Add the onion and cook gently for 5–10 minutes, until soft.

Add the mushrooms to the frying pan and stir-fry for a few minutes, until they begin to soften. Stir in the tomato purée and mustard, then add the crème fraîche. Cook gently, stirring constantly, for 5 minutes.

Stir in the paprika and season to taste with salt and pepper. Garnish with extra paprika and parsley sprigs and serve immediately.

Serves 4

25 g/1 oz butter

1 onion, finely chopped

450 g/1 lb closed-cup mushrooms, quartered

1 tsp tomato purée

1 tsp coarse grain mustard

150 ml/5 fl oz crème fraîche

1 tsp paprika, plus extra to garnish

salt and pepper

fresh flat-leaf parsley sprigs, to garnish

SPICY VEGETABLE LASAGNE

Place the aubergine slices in a colander, sprinkle with salt and leave for 20 minutes. Rinse under cold water, drain and reserve.

Preheat the oven to 180°C/350°F/Gas Mark 4. Heat the oil in a saucepan. Add the garlic and onion and sauté for 1–2 minutes. Add the peppers, mushrooms, celery and courgette and cook, stirring constantly, for 3–4 minutes.

Stir in the chilli powder and cumin and cook for 1 minute. Mix in the tomatoes, passata and 2 tablespoons of the basil and season to taste with salt and pepper.

For the sauce, melt the butter in a saucepan. Stir in the flour and cook for 1 minute. Remove from the heat, gradually stir in the stock and milk, return to the heat, then add half the cheese and all the mustard. Boil, stirring, until thickened. Stir in the remaining basil. Remove from the heat and stir in the egg.

Place half the lasagne sheets in an ovenproof dish. Top with half the vegetable and tomato sauce, then half the aubergines. Repeat and then spoon the cheese sauce on top. Sprinkle with the remaining cheese and bake in the preheated oven for 40 minutes, or until golden and bubbling.

CASHEW NUT PAELLA

Heat the oil and butter in a large frying pan or paella pan until the butter has melted.

Add the onion and cook over a medium heat, stirring constantly, for 2–3 minutes, until softened.

Stir in the rice, turmeric, cumin, chilli powder, garlic, chilli, green and red peppers, baby corn, olives and tomato and cook over a medium heat, stirring occasionally, for 1–2 minutes.

Pour in the stock and bring the mixture to the boil. Reduce the heat and cook gently, stirring constantly, for a further 20 minutes.

Add the cashew nuts and peas and continue to cook, stirring occasionally, for a further 5 minutes. Season to taste with salt and pepper and add the parsley and a pinch of cayenne pepper. Transfer the paella to warm serving plates and serve immediately.

Serves 4

2 tbsp olive oil

1 tbsp butter

1 red onion, chopped

150 g/5½ oz arborio rice

1 tsp ground turmeric

1 tsp ground cumin

½ tsp chilli powder

3 garlic cloves, crushed

1 fresh green chilli, deseeded and sliced

1 green pepper, deseeded and diced

1 red pepper, deseeded and diced

85 g/3 oz baby corn, halved lengthways

2 tbsp stoned black olives

1 large tomato, deseeded and diced

450 ml/16 fl oz vegetable stock

85 g/3 oz unsalted cashew nuts

55 g/2 oz frozen peas

2 tbsp chopped fresh parsley

pinch of cayenne pepper

salt and pepper

CATALAN STUFFED PEPPERS

Serves 4

280 g/10 oz basmati rice

300 g/10 oz baby spinach leaves, rinsed

2 tbsp olive oil

1 small onion, finely chopped

2 large garlic cloves, crushed

1/4 tsp ground turmeric

large pinch of ground cinnamon

large pinch of cayenne pepper, or to taste

4 tbsp pine kernels, toasted

4 tbsp raisins

4 large peppers, any colour

salt and pepper

Put the rice in a sieve and rinse under cold running water until the water runs clear. Transfer to a bowl, cover with water and leave to soak for at least 30 minutes.

Put the spinach in a large pan with just the water clinging to the leaves, cover and cook over a medium heat until it has wilted. Drain well, and when cool enough to handle squeeze out all the water. Chop finely and set aside.

Meanwhile, preheat the oven to 180°C/350°F/Gas Mark 4. Heat 1 tablespoon of the oil in a large frying pan over a medium heat. Add the onion and stir for 5 minutes or until soft. Add the garlic, turmeric, cinnamon and cayenne pepper and stir for 2 minutes.

Stir in the pine kernels, raisins and drained rice. Add the chopped spinach and stir together, then season to taste with salt and pepper. Set aside.

Cut each pepper in half lengthways, and then carefully remove the cores and seeds. Take care not to cut away the stem ends. Divide the rice stuffing equally between the the pepper halves, and then arrange them in 1–2 large roasting tins that support them tightly.

Bake in the preheated oven for 45 minutes–1 hour and serve immediately.

197

CARROT & PUMPKIN CURRY

Pour the stock into a large saucepan and bring to the boil. Add the galangal, half the garlic, the lemon grass and chillies and simmer for 5 minutes. Add the carrots and pumpkin and simmer for 5–6 minutes, until tender.

Meanwhile, heat the oil in a wok or frying pan and stir-fry the shallots and the remaining garlic for 2–3 minutes. Add the curry paste and stir-fry for 1–2 minutes.

Stir the shallot mixture into the saucepan and add the coconut milk and Thai basil. Simmer for 2–3 minutes. Serve hot, sprinkled with the toasted pumpkin seeds.

Serves 4

150 ml/5 fl oz vegetable stock

2.5-cm/1-inch piece fresh galangal, sliced

2 garlic cloves, chopped

1 lemon grass stalk (white part only), finely chopped

2 fresh red chillies, deseeded and chopped

4 carrots, peeled and cut into chunks

225 g/8 oz pumpkin, peeled, deseeded and cut into cubes

2 tbsp vegetable or groundnut oil

2 shallots, finely chopped

3 tbsp Thai yellow curry paste

400 ml/14 fl oz coconut milk

4–6 fresh Thai basil sprigs

25 g/1 oz toasted pumpkin seeds, to garnish

AUBERGINE & POTATO CURRY

Quarter the aubergine lengthways and cut into 5-cm/2-inch pieces. Soak the aubergine pieces in cold water.

Peel the potatoes and cut into 5-cm/2-inch cubes. Heat the oil in a large saucepan over a medium heat. When hot, add the mustard seeds and, as soon as they start popping, add the nigella seeds and fennel seeds.

Add the onion, ginger and chillies and cook for 7–8 minutes, until the mixture begins to brown.

Add the cumin, ground coriander, turmeric and chilli powder. Cook for about a minute, then add the tomato purée. Cook for a further minute, pour in the warm water, then add the salt and aubergine. Bring to the boil and cook over a medium heat for 8–10 minutes, stirring frequently to ensure that the aubergine cooks evenly. At the start of cooking, the aubergine will float, but once it soaks up the liquid it will sink. As soon as the aubergine sinks, add the potatoes and cook for 2–3 minutes, stirring.

Stir in the garam masala and chopped coriander and remove from the heat. Serve with Indian bread.

GREEN BEAN & POTATO CURRY

▼▼▼▼▼▼▼▼▼▼▼▼▼▼▼▼▼▼▼▼▼

Heat the oil in a large heavy-based saucepan. Add the white cumin seeds, mustard and onion seeds and dried red chillies, stirring well.

Add the tomatoes to the pan and stir-fry the mixture for 3–5 minutes.

Mix the salt, ginger, garlic and chilli powder together in a bowl and spoon into the saucepan. Blend the whole mixture together.

Add the green beans and potatoes to the saucepan and stir-fry for 5 minutes.

Add the water to the saucepan, reduce the heat and simmer for 10–15 minutes, stirring occasionally. Transfer to a warmed serving dish, garnish with chopped coriander and green chillies and serve.

Serves 6

300 ml/10 fl oz vegetable oil

1 tsp white cumin seeds

1 tsp mixed mustard and onion seeds

4 dried red chillies

3 fresh tomatoes, sliced

1 tsp salt

1 tsp finely chopped fresh ginger

1 tsp crushed fresh garlic

1 tsp chilli powder

200 g/7 oz green beans, diagonally sliced into 2.5-cm/1-inch lengths

2 potatoes, peeled and diced

300 ml/10 fl oz water

chopped fresh coriander and finely sliced green chillies, to garnish

SPICED BASMATI PILAU

Serves 4

500 g/1 lb 2 oz basmati rice

175 g/6 oz head of broccoli

6 tbsp vegetable oil

2 large onions, chopped

225 g/8 oz mushrooms, sliced

2 garlic cloves, crushed

6 green cardamom pods, split

6 whole cloves

8 black peppercorns

1 cinnamon stick or piece of cassia bark

1 tsp ground turmeric

1.2 litres/2 pints vegetable stock or water

60 g/2¼ oz seedless raisins

60 g/2¼ oz unsalted pistachio nuts, roughly chopped

salt and pepper

Place the rice in a sieve and rinse under cold running water. Drain. Trim off most of the broccoli stalk and cut the head into small florets, then quarter the stalk lengthways and cut diagonally into 1-cm/½-inch pieces.

Heat the oil in a large saucepan. Add the onions and broccoli stalk and cook over a low heat, stirring frequently, for 3 minutes. Add the mushrooms, rice, garlic and spices and cook for 1 minute, stirring, until the rice is coated in oil.

Add the stock and season to taste with salt and pepper. Stir in the broccoli florets and return the mixture to the boil. Cover, reduce the heat and cook over a low heat for 15 minutes without uncovering the pan.

Remove the pan from the heat and leave the pilau to stand for 5 minutes without uncovering. Remove and discard the whole spices, add the raisins and pistachio nuts and gently fork through to fluff up the grains. Serve the pilau hot.

BROWN RICE VEGETABLE PILAU

Heat 2 tablespoons of the oil in a deep frying pan with a lid over a medium heat. Add the onion. Cook for 5 minutes, or until softened.

Add the celery, carrots, chilli, spring onions and almonds. Stir-fry for 2 minutes, or until the vegetables are tender but still firm to the bite, and still brightly coloured. Transfer to a bowl and reserve until required.

Add the remaining oil to the frying pan. Stir in the rice and lentils. Cook over a medium–high heat, stirring, for 1–2 minutes, or until heated through. Reduce the heat. Stir in the stock and orange juice. Season to taste with salt and pepper.

Return the vegetables to the frying pan. Toss with the rice for a few minutes, until heated through. Transfer to a warmed dish and serve.

Serves 4

4 tbsp vegetable oil

1 red onion, finely chopped

2 tender celery sticks, leaves included, quartered lengthways and diced

2 carrots, coarsely grated

1 fresh green chilli, deseeded and finely chopped

3 spring onions, green parts included, finely chopped

40 g/1½ oz whole almonds, sliced lengthways

350 g/12 oz cooked brown basmati rice

150 g/5½ oz cooked split red lentils

175 ml/6 fl oz chicken stock or vegetable stock

5 tbsp freshly squeezed orange juice

salt and pepper

VEGETABLE STIR-FRY SALAD

Heat the oil in a preheated wok, add the spring onions, ginger and lemon grass and stir-fry over a medium-high heat for 2–3 minutes, until starting to soften. Add the carrots, broccoli and baby corn and stir-fry for 3–4 minutes, until starting to soften. Add the water chestnuts and curry paste and stir well, then stir-fry for a further 2–3 minutes. Discard the lemon grass.

Meanwhile, cook the noodles in a large saucepan of lightly salted boiling water for 4–5 minutes, or according to the packet instructions, until just tender. Drain and return to the saucepan. Add the sesame seeds and toss to coat.

Add the noodles to the stir-fried vegetables and serve immediately.

VEGETABLES WITH TOFU & SPINACH

Heat the oil for deep-frying in a preheated wok, deep saucepan or deep-fat fryer to 180–190°C/350–375°F, or until a cube of bread browns in 30 seconds. Add the tofu cubes, in batches, and cook for 4–5 minutes, until crisp and brown all over. Remove with a slotted spoon and drain on kitchen paper.

Heat the 2 tablespoons of oil in a wok or frying pan and stir-fry the onions, garlic and chilli for 1–2 minutes, until they start to soften. Add the celery, mushrooms, baby corn and red pepper and stir-fry for 3–4 minutes, until they soften.

Stir in the curry paste and coconut milk and gradually bring to the boil. Add the sugar and soy sauce and then the spinach. Cook, stirring constantly, until the spinach has wilted. Serve immediately, topped with the tofu.

Serves 4

vegetable or groundnut oil, for deep-frying

225 g/8 oz firm tofu, drained and cut into cubes

2 tbsp vegetable or groundnut oil

2 onions, chopped

2 garlic cloves, chopped

1 fresh red chilli, deseeded and sliced

3 celery sticks, diagonally sliced

225 g/8 oz mushrooms, thickly sliced

115 g/4 oz baby corn, cut in half

1 red pepper, deseeded and cut into strips

3 tbsp Thai red curry paste

400 ml/14 fl oz coconut milk

1 tsp palm sugar or soft light brown sugar

2 tbsp Thai soy sauce

225 g/8 oz baby spinach leaves

VEGETARIAN CHILLI BURGERS

Serves 4–6

85 g/3 oz bulgar wheat

300 g/10½ oz canned red kidney beans, drained and rinsed

300 g/10½ oz canned cannellini beans, drained

1–2 fresh red jalapeño chillies, deseeded and roughly chopped

2–3 garlic cloves

6 spring onions, roughly chopped

1 yellow pepper, deseeded, peeled and chopped

1 tbsp chopped fresh coriander

115 g/4 oz mature Cheddar cheese, grated

2 tbsp wholemeal flour

1–2 tbsp sunflower oil

1 large tomato, sliced

salt and pepper

wholemeal buns, to serve

Place the bulgar wheat in a sieve and rinse under cold running water. Cook the bulgar wheat in a saucepan of lightly salted water for 12 minutes, or until tender. Drain and reserve.

Place the beans in a food processor with the chillies, garlic, spring onions, yellow pepper, coriander and half the cheese. Using the pulse button, chop finely. Add to the cooked bulgar wheat with salt and pepper to taste. Mix well, then shape into 4–6 equal-sized burgers. Cover and leave to chill for 1 hour. Coat the burgers in the flour.

Preheat the grill to medium. Heat a heavy-based frying pan and add the oil. When hot, add the burgers and cook over a medium heat for 5–6 minutes on each side, or until piping hot.

Place 1–2 slices of tomato on top of each burger and sprinkle with the remaining cheese. Cook under the hot grill for 2–3 minutes, or until the cheese begins to melt. Serve in wholemeal buns.

213

PUMPKIN PARCELS WITH CHILLI & LIME

Preheat the barbecue or preheat the oven to 190°C/375°C/Gas Mark 5. Halve the pumpkin and scoop out the seeds. Rinse the seeds and reserve. Cut the pumpkin into thin wedges and peel.

Heat the oil and butter together in a large saucepan, stirring, until melted. Stir in the chilli sauce, lime rind and juice. Add the pumpkin and seeds to the saucepan and toss to coat on all sides in the flavoured butter.

Divide the mixture among 4 double-thickness sheets of foil. Fold over the foil to enclose the pumpkin mixture completely.

Cook the foil parcels over hot coals or in the preheated oven for 15–25 minutes, or until the pumpkin is tender. Transfer the foil parcels to warmed serving plates. Open the parcels at the table and serve immediately.

Serves 4

700 g/1 lb 9 oz pumpkin or squash
2 tbsp sunflower oil
25 g/1 oz butter
½ tsp chilli sauce
grated rind of 1 lime
2 tsp lime juice

PASTA ALL' ARRABBIATA

To make the sugocasa, heat the oil in a frying pan over a high heat until almost smoking. Add the tomatoes and cook, stirring frequently, for 2–3 minutes. Reduce the heat to low and cook gently for 20 minutes, or until very soft. Season to taste with salt and pepper. Using a wooden spoon, press through a non-metallic sieve into a saucepan.

Add the wine, sun-dried tomato purée, whole chillies and garlic to the sugocasa and bring to the boil. Reduce the heat and simmer gently.

Meanwhile, bring a large saucepan of lightly salted water to the boil. Add the pasta, return to the boil and cook for 8–10 minutes, until the pasta is tender but still firm to the bite.

Remove the chillies and taste the sauce. If you prefer a hotter flavour, chop some or all of the chillies and return to the saucepan. Check and adjust the seasoning, adding salt and pepper if necessary, then stir in half the parsley.

Drain the pasta and transfer to a warmed serving bowl. Add the sauce and toss to coat. Sprinkle with the remaining parsley, garnish with the cheese shavings and serve at once.

CHILLI BROCCOLI PASTA

Bring a large saucepan of lightly salted water to the boil, add the pasta and cook for about 10 minutes, until the pasta is tender but still firm to the bite. Remove from the heat, drain, rinse with cold water and drain again. Set aside.

Cut the broccoli into florets. Bring a saucepan of lightly salted water to the boil, add the broccoli and cook for 5 minutes. Drain, rinse with cold water and drain again.

Heat the oil in the pan that the pasta was cooked in. Add the garlic, chillies and tomatoes, if using. Cook over a high heat for 1 minute.

Add the broccoli to the pan and mix well. Cook for 2 minutes to heat through. Add the pasta and mix well again. Cook for a further minute.

Remove the pasta from the heat, tip into a large serving bowl and serve, garnished with the basil.

Serves 4

225 g/8 oz dried penne or macaroni

225 g/8 oz head of broccoli

50 ml/2 fl oz extra virgin olive oil

2 large garlic cloves, chopped

2 fresh red chillies, deseeded and diced

8 cherry tomatoes, halved (optional)

salt

small handful of fresh chopped basil or parsley, to garnish

CHILLI TOFU TORTILLAS

Makes 8

½ tsp chilli powder

1 tsp paprika

2 tbsp plain flour

225 g/8 oz firm tofu, cut into 1-cm/½-inch pieces

2 tbsp vegetable oil

1 onion, finely chopped

1 garlic clove, crushed

1 large red pepper, deseeded and finely chopped

1 large ripe avocado

1 tbsp lime juice

4 tomatoes, peeled, deseeded and chopped

125 g/4½ oz Cheddar cheese, grated

8 flour tortillas

150 ml/5 fl oz soured cream

850 ml/1½ pints sugocasa

3 tbsp chopped fresh parsley

3 tbsp chopped fresh coriander

salt and pepper

pickled green jalapeño chillies, to serve

Preheat the oven to 190°C/375°F/Gas Mark 5. Mix the chilli powder, paprika, flour, and salt and pepper to taste on a plate and use to coat the tofu pieces.

Heat the oil in a frying pan and gently fry the tofu for 3–4 minutes, until golden. Remove with a slotted spoon, drain on kitchen paper and set aside.

Add the onion, garlic and red pepper to the oil and fry for 2–3 minutes, until just soft. Drain and set aside.

Halve the avocado, peel and remove the stone. Slice lengthways, put in a bowl with the lime juice and toss to coat. Add the tofu and the onion mixture and gently stir in the tomatoes and half the cheese. Spoon an eighth of the filling down the centre of each tortilla, top with soured cream and roll up. Arrange the tortillas in a single layer in a shallow ovenproof dish.

Mix the sugocasa, parsley and coriander together in a bowl. Spoon over the tortillas, sprinkle with the remaining grated cheese and bake in the preheated oven for 25 minutes, until the cheese is golden brown and bubbling.

Serve the tortillas immediately with the pickled jalapeño chillies.

Index

223